The
Reference Shelf ®

Affordable Housing

The Reference Shelf
Volume 91 • Number 2
H.W. Wilson
A Division of EBSCO Information Services, Inc.

Published by
GREY HOUSE PUBLISHING
Amenia, New York
2019

The Reference Shelf

The books in this series contain reprints of articles, excerpts from books, addresses on current issues, and studies of social trends in the United States and other countries. There are six separately bound numbers in each volume, all of which are usually published in the same calendar year. Numbers one through five are each devoted to a single subject, providing background information and discussion from various points of view and concluding with an index and comprehensive bibliography that lists books, pamphlets, and articles on the subject. The final number of each volume is a collection of recent speeches. Books in the series may be purchased individually or on subscription.

Publisher's Cataloging-In-Publication Data
(Prepared by The Donohue Group, Inc.)

Names: Grey House Publishing, Inc., compiler, publisher.

Title: Affordable housing / [compiled by Grey House Publishing].

Other Titles: Reference shelf ; v. 91, no. 2.

Description: Amenia, New York : Grey House Publishing, 2019. | Includes bibliographical references and index.

Identifiers: ISBN 9781642652192 (v. 91, no. 2) | ISBN 9781642652178 (volume set)

Subjects: LCSH: Housing--United States--Costs--Sources. | Public housing--United States--Sources. | Residential real estate--United States--Sources. | Home ownership--United States--Sources. | Mortgages--United States--Sources.

Classification: LCC HD7293 .A74 2019 | DDC 363.596230973--dc23

Printed in Canada

Contents

3

Exploring the Affordable Housing Debate

4

Housing and Welfare

5

Possible Solutions

Preface

Homes for All

Affordable housing means different things to different people. For some, the idea of affordable housing is a cornerstone of social welfare, an effort to provide the greatest number of people possible with the capability to own or lease a home or apartment without sacrificing economic stability. At its most ideal, affordable housing advocates claim that access to functional, affordable housing should be a basic human right, guaranteed by government revenues or whatever system is necessary to ensure that no one is left unable to afford this most basic foundation of human prosperity. For others, affordable housing amounts to little more than a series of failed governmental efforts to regulate and subsidize the housing market, which some argue has done more harm than good. At times, politicians and housing advocates speak of affordable housing as if it is an independent issue, but it is more realistically conceptualized as part of the broader debate over income and economic inequality.

A Characteristic American Problem

The effort to create or ensure access to affordable housing is far from a new feature of American society. Beginning in the late 1800s, a few American towns and cities were already beginning to see a problem as housing development rapidly outpaced affordability for those at the lower end of the income spectrum. The federal government's initial foray into affordable housing was in the form of subsidized housing programs built specifically for low-income individuals and families. In the 1960s and '70s, the federal government changed directions and began focusing on public-private partnerships in which companies, both nonprofit and for-profit, were contracted to build and maintain low cost housing.[1]

New affordable housing programs accompanied the most tumultuous periods in American history. Following World War I and World War II, there were efforts to create affordable housing in part motivated by public calls to help poor veterans and their families. The Great Depression introduced Americans across the income spectrum to the problems of poverty and homelessness like never before. The Depression made Americans realize that even those at the upper end of the income spectrum were not invulnerable to shifting economic patterns and it helped average Americans to see the connections between the income classes that tie the economy together. With middle- and upper-class individuals and families suddenly finding themselves with the same standing as low-income workers, public support for government intervention peaked, leading to one of the most significant expansions of social welfare programs in American history. In the 1960s and '70s, the focus in affordable housing changed again, embracing the prevailing efforts to address racial and class prejudice that had long hindered certain potential renters and homeowners from entering the market. Another resurgence in affordable housing reform followed the Great Recession of 2007-2010, the economic impact of which still affects the lives of many Americans at various levels of the income spectrum.[2]

Though economic growth is strong in 2019, America still has a severe housing crisis. Estimates from 2017 and 2018 indicate that nearly half of all renters in America are "rent-burdened," spending over one-third—the demarcation line that marks housing as affordable by most current standards—of their total income on housing. The Urban Institute estimated in 2018 that one in four renters in rural areas spent more than 50 percent of their income on housing. With rising real estate costs, far surpassing the costs of construction, the lack of affordable housing is also expanding, impacting individuals in the middle-income markets as well as those earning low income. Harvard University's Joint Center for Housing Studies estimated in 2017 that the US housing market was the least affordable in the last decade. Further, America's homelessness rate grew in 2017 and 2018 for the first time in a decade, a phenomenon that is, in part, reflective of the ongoing impact of the Great Recession of the 2000s.[3]

A Varied Landscape

Among the issues affecting housing affordability, activists and politicians have identified zoning and land-use regulations as among the most important. In many areas, zoning and land-use limitations restrict development and, in some cases, directly prevent the construction of affordable units within certain areas. The most popular solutions for affordable housing among fiscal conservatives is to reduce regulation, essentially relying on supply and demand to solve the problem as developers initiate more affordable housing projects to meet demand. However, voters in many areas object to the idea of lifting land-use restrictions, concerned about how unrestrained development might change their communities.[4] Some progressive activists want federal intervention, either to regulate the private sector or to engage, directly, in creating new housing. Critics of this approach point to the failure of past government efforts, doubting the effectiveness of federal intervention. Others perceive a need for federal management, at least, to ensure that states and private companies are considering public welfare when creating and enforcing housing policies. Some believe that the federal government should subsidize families directly, utilizing public funds to enable individuals and families in need to occupy units that might otherwise be outside of their means.

Debates about affordable housing have been complicated by the fact that America's housing crisis has a distinctly regional character. In some areas, the housing problem is so severe that low- to middle-income renters and potential homeowners are forced to search for housing far from productive city centers, adding the cost of long commutes to their expenses. In some areas, there is a clear lack of available units, while in others units are available but priced too high for renters or potential buyers who aren't in upper income percentiles. Because the housing issue differs across regions, and because available resources differ from region to region, solutions need to be tailored to each individual area.[5]

In some cases, towns and cities have enacted their own measures to address the problem. Many have adopted inclusive zoning requirements, which require developers to set aside a certain proportion of their development for affordable housing. This approach is popular with many politicians, as it shifts the burden for funding to private companies and makes affordable housing part of the cost of otherwise lucrative building projects within popular areas. However, loopholes in local laws enable companies to avoid contributing to affordable housing and, in other cases, the affordable units set aside under inclusive zoning projects are still too expensive to help low-income individuals. Other cities and towns have adopted more unusual measures. For instance, the cities of Denver and Pittsburgh have both created regional housing loan funds that are used specifically to fund affordable housing projects from developers. Affordable housing advocates have pointed to Denver's unique housing loan program as a prime example of "holistic development" because of the way the city has integrated plans for housing into other local development initiatives. For instance, Denver plans to locate new affordable housing projects alongside the city's light-rail system, thereby offering potential residents both affordability and inexpensive options for transportation.[6]

While regional solutions can be effective and innovative, not all communities can afford to initiate their own affordable housing solutions, and not all governments have the will or desire to address this issue. Affordable housing also dovetails into many other highly sensitive issues impacting social welfare, such as racism and class prejudice, factors that have played a role in the formation of local housing policies and patterns of exclusion and availability. Individuals and communities often resist affordable housing projects in their immediate area, whether out of concern about property values, the perceived risk of crime, or simply out of a desire to preserve the familiar aesthetics and demographics of their communities.

On the public welfare side of the equation, America is coping with a homelessness crisis that is directly related to the affordable housing problem. Homelessness rates have expanded in 2017 and 2018, indicating worsening conditions for both renters and buyers in many communities and reflecting a reduced focus on social welfare under President Donald Trump's administration. Opinions on homelessness also run the gamut. While some believe that homelessness can be solved by jobs or job training, experts in the field disagree. The availability of secure housing is a necessity for physical and psychological stability, a prerequisite for individuals to look for work and to improve conditions for their families.[7]

Housing and Economic Inequality

Affordable housing is just one of a number of modern debates related to one of America's most pressing problems: income inequality. Income inequality refers to the gap in earnings between those at the top and those at the bottom. Most Americans are familiar with the "ultra-rich," the few who sit at the very top of the income spectrum with assets ranging into the billions and, at times, control of the most influential companies in the country or even the world. The very first super-rich Americans emerged during the Industrial Revolution and capitalized on the "tech trends" of the day, like railroads, coal mining, and industrialized timber harvesting. These celebrated and maligned "Captains of Industry" represent for some the ultimate manifestation of the American dream, the accrual of personal wealth. Others see these individuals as profiteers who manipulated a fundamentally unequal system and exploited the poor and working class to build their fortunes while ignoring the welfare of those workers.

The Great Depression narrowed the gap between the rich and the poor, but development since has reinstated and widened the income gulf. Since the Great Recession, inequality has risen faster than ever, with the wealth gap affecting an ever-widening pool of American workers. In 2015, it was estimated that the top 1 percent of families in the United States earned more than 25 times more than everyone in the remaining 99 percent. Income at the top 1 percent has also grown faster than in the bottom 99 percent, to the point that most Americans have gradually lost purchasing power and real wealth, which has increasingly become concentrated among the very rich. Pay for chief executive officers (CEOs) was about 20 times higher than the average company worker in 1965 while, by 2016 the average CEO earned 271 times what the average worker earned. In New York, earners at the top 1 percent had an average salary of over 2 million, while the average salary for those in the remaining 99 percent was just over $49,000.[8]

This income disparity affects affordable housing in ways both obvious and subtle. It can be argued that wealth on this extreme scale cannot be achieved solely on the basis of individual effort, ingenuity, or intelligence. Achieving income on this level requires the participation of individuals at every level of the income spectrum, many of whom work more hours and in more physically demanding work than those at the top tiers of a company. A real estate company's success also hinges on the work of janitors, custodians, construction workers, property managers, sales associates, receptionists, and many others whose level of compensation does not necessarily reflect their effort or time. Further, whether or not a developer is able to attract tenants or buyers depends on the neighborhood in which the development is situated, and this means that success is dependent on the broader functionality of the city. Without roads, police, public utilities, and other municipal amenities, businesses couldn't function. Attracting customers might also depend on the racial, ethnic, and class composition of a city or community, as well as the presence or absence of things like schools, public transportation, retail grocery shopping, and entertainment venues. The success of a real-estate business depends on the effort of many who create the communities in which a specific real-estate development might succeed.

Some believe that companies and individuals should be permitted to accrue unlimited personal or corporate wealth, while others believe that the profits of a company's success should be more evenly distributed. In the realm of housing, this philosophical debate includes such questions as whether or not companies have a responsibility to engage in projects based not only on the pursuit of profit but also on the needs and welfare of others in the community. When debating issues like income inequality, wage stagnation, and affordable housing, those on both sides are essentially asking Americans to consider what we, as members of a community, a city, a state, and a country, owe to one another. Should America preserve the potential for individual achievement at the cost of the welfare of others, or should America strive to redistribute the wealth accumulated through collective productivity? In housing, should our communities be responsible for sharing the fruits of corporate and personal success such that as many people as possible can achieve the fundamental benefits of a safe and affordable home?

Micah L. Issitt

Works Used

Calhoun, Michael. "Lessons from the Financial Crisis: The Central Importance of a Sustainable, Affordable and Inclusive Housing Market." *Brookings*. The Brookings Insitution. Sep 5, 2018. Retrieved from https://www.brookings.edu/research/lessons-from-the-financial-crisis-the-central-importance-of-a-sustainable-affordable-and-inclusive-housing-market/.

Florida, Richard. "How Affordable Housing Can Improve the American Economy." *CityLab*. Feb 5, 2019. Retrieved from https://www.citylab.com/life/2019/02/affordable-housing-economy-city-zoning-home-prices/582022/.

Kneebone, Elizabeth, Snyderman, Robin and Cecile Murray. "Advancing Regional Solutions to Address America's Housing Affordability Crisis." *Brookings*. The Brookings Institution. Oct 23, 2017 Retrieved from https://www.brookings.edu/blog/the-avenue/2017/10/19/advancing-regional-solutions-to-address-americas-housing-affordability-crisis/.

Ligon, John. "Federal Reforms Should Include Housing and Land-Use Deregulation." *Heritage*. The Heritage Foundation. Mar 28, 2018. Retrieved from https://www.heritage.org/housing/report/federal-reforms-should-include-housing-and-land-use-deregulation.

Reinicke, Carmen. "US Income Inequality Continues to Grow." *CNBC*. CNBC. Jul 19, 2018. Retrieved from https://www.cnbc.com/2018/07/19/income-inequality-continues-to-grow-in-the-united-states.html.

Sisson, Patrick. "Solving Affordable Housing: Creative Solutions Around the U.S." *Curbed*. Vox Media. Jul 25, 2017. Retrieved from https://www.curbed.com/2017/7/25/16020648/affordable-housing-apartment-urban-development.

Von Hoffman, Alexander. "To Preserve Affordable Housing in the United States: A Policy History." *JCHS*. Joint Center for Housing Studies. March 2016, retrieved from http://www.jchs.harvard.edu/sites/default/files/von_hoffman_to_preserve_affordable_housing_april16.pdf.

Wiltz, Teresa. "As Affordable Housing Crisis Deepens, States Begin to Take Action." *CS Monitor*. Oct 16, 2018. Retrieved from https://www.csmonitor.com/Business/2018/1016/As-affordable-housing-crisis-deepens-states-begin-to-take-action.

Notes

1. Von Hoffman, "To Preserve Affordable Housing in the United States: A Policy History."
2. Calhoun, "Lessons from the Financial Crisis: The Central Importance of a Sustainable, Affordable and Inclusive Housing Market."
3. Wiltz, "As Affordable Housing Crisis Deepens, States Begin to Take Action."
4. Ligon, "Federal Reforms Should Include Housing and Land-Use Deregulation."
5. Kneebone, Snyderman, Murray, "Advancing Regional Solutions to Address America's Housing Affordability Crisis."
6. Sisson, "Solving Affordable Housing: Creative Solutions around the U.S."
7. Florida, "How Affordable Housing Can Improve the American Economy."
8. Reinicke, "US Income Inequality Continues to Grow."

1
The Housing Crisis

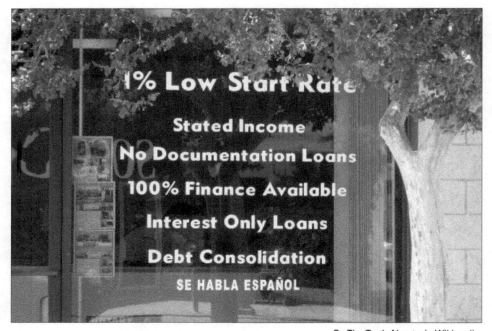

By The Truth About, via Wikimedia.

The 2007-2008 financial crisis had a major effect on affordable housing in the United States, and its effects are still being felt. Above, a mortgage brokerage advertises subprime mortgages in July 2008.

How Did We Get Here?

There is widespread agreement among economists and housing industry experts that the United States has a housing crisis. However, the nature of the housing crisis differs from region to region, state to state, and community to community. While activists and politicians have attempted to call attention to the issue, housing is not a top priority at the upper levels of American politics. However, given the increasing severity of the problem and its potential to impact more and more Americans, it is possible that affordable housing could become a central public policy issues in coming years.

A Political Debate?

In the tumultuous years since Donald Trump was elected president, the issue of housing has been all but lost from the federal perspective. Despite the fact that income and housing inequality are pressing issues in many states, little attention has been given to them in public or in governmental circles. And many, if not most Americans, are at best marginally aware of any existing housing problem. In a May 2018 article in *CityLab*, Michael Franzini, founder of Public Interest (a nonprofit advertising agency), explained that his company was seeking to bring the issue of housing policy into the public debate in a similar way to how Al Gore brought greater public awareness to the issue of climate change in the 2000s. To achieve this, Public Interest created the "Home1" campaign, consisting of a series of modern public service messages designed to be transmitted through social media, with plans to develop a feature documentary on the issue for streaming services. As Franzini told *CityLab*, "There is no greater crisis that, at least in my lifetime, has ever faced our country and not been talked about."[1]

In a 2016 article for the National Center for Housing Management, president Glenn Stevens, frustrated by the lack of attention given to the issue during the 2016 presidential and legislative campaigns (during which time affordable housing was never mentioned in any of the presidential debates), summarized the current state of the housing problem. With over 48 million Americans at or below the poverty level, and only 5 million HUD-supported housing units available, Stevens explained that 7 million Americans were contending with a constant "housing bubble" that, in some parts of the country, had reached epidemic proportions. Citing one example, Stevens notes that in 2015 the Housing Authority of Baltimore opened their waiting list for subsidized housing for a period of only three days, receiving 75,000 applicants, 50,000 of whom were turned away.[2]

Some might wonder whether the strong economic growth frequently mentioned by GOP political candidates and spokespeople for the Trump administration might eventually help to alleviate the affordable housing issue, but this is unlikely to be the case. Affordable housing is directly related to growing income inequality in the United States. A Pew Research report in August of 2018 demonstrated that, for the vast majority of Americans, real wages have not increased for nearly two decades. Much of the nation's economic growth in this period has benefitted only those at the upper end of the income spectrum. The cost of living, meanwhile, has increased in concert with spending at the upper level of the income spectrum. It is increasingly difficult for middle- and low-income families and individuals to afford health-care, food, education, and housing.[3] The most recent round of tax reforms proposed under the Trump administration benefited wealthy individuals and corporations. According to supporters, the extra income and earnings created by these tax cuts will filter through society as companies and upper-income consumers will create more jobs. Critics argue that this "trickle down" theory does not work in practice and merely benefits a small portion of America's consumers and earners, while doing little for the majority of Americans.

The Depth of the Issue

Drawing on the 2018 Harvard University report from the Joint Center for Housing Studies, *Huffington Post* reporter Michael Hobbes provides a grim assessment, arguing that the housing sector is, by many different metrics of evaluation, dysfunctional and becoming more so. While median earnings increased by only 5 percent between 1960 and 2018, rental prices have gone up 61 percent. Among homeowners, earnings have increased by as much as 50 percent, but housing costs have increased by more than 112 percent. Meanwhile, the JCHS report indicated that the private real estate industry is responsible for perpetuating the patterns that lead to housing insecurity. Developers exploit poverty-stricken areas, displacing residents, which leads to sprawl, pushing affordable housing into economically compromised areas. Further, housing costs are rising faster at the lower end of the spectrum, which means that individuals and families are increasingly being priced out while housing prices remain stable at the upper levels, where income is still increasing. Hobbes summarized the problem, writing, "The housing crisis is the ticking time bomb at the heart of the American economy, wiping savings, increasing inequality and reducing the ability of workers to weather the next recession."[4]

Franzini's Public Interest has drawn together some of the more impactful statistics about the current issue for their Home1 PSAs. In one, called "The Silent Crisis In America," Public Interest explains that one out of every three American families rents their home while the supply of rental properties has declined, driving up prices for remaining units. Approximately one in four of those who rent spend more than 50 percent of their income on rent alone. Further, three quarters of the American population has less than $1000 in savings, and a full one-third have no savings at all. For these individuals, Public Interest explains, any family crisis, such as a medical issue, missed paycheck, or car repair, can essentially put them on the verge of homelessness. In 2018, 315,617 Americans were evicted, with one person being evicted approximately every 11 seconds across the nation. That the housing issue is an emergency is justified by citing the fact that even individuals in competitive jobs that take years of specialized training, such as paramedics and EMTs, are unable to afford decent properties.[5]

Some of the economists and other specialists evaluating America's housing issues have pointed to the Great Recession of 2007-2010 as a significant contributor. It has been difficult for many families and individuals to recover from the recession, which compromised credit and created debt for many Americans at various income levels, and many of those who lost their houses during the recession have been unable to return to ownership. While the Recession provides an example of macro-level economic shifts that have marginalized many potential renters and home buyers, economic turmoil at the state, municipal, or community level can likewise impact the ability of consumers to access affordable housing options or to attain sufficient capital to enter the increasingly expensive rental and home buying markets.

Furthermore, individuals investigating the housing issue have found that zoning and land-use regulations, put into place by individuals seeking to maintain a certain character for their communities, exacerbate and, in some cases, are the key variable preventing individuals from finding homes or rental properties. Studies continue to show that housing and rental shortages disproportionately impact the poor, America's racial minorities, and individuals marginalized by medical or educational debt. America's cities, long a bastion for workers in the mid- to lower classes, have become increasingly expensive while wages have not increased, thus driving residents into sprawling suburbs where economic opportunities are rare and from which they face the burden of longer commutes while the cost of vehicles and transportation also increases.[6] While some argue that higher real estate costs reflect the increasing costs encountered by the real estate industry, research by economist Joseph Gyourko and colleagues has helped to demonstrate that the cost of constructing houses and rental units has risen only slightly since 1980, while the cost of purchasing houses has more than quadrupled over the same time period.[7]

Studies also indicate that the problem is highly geographic, with housing shortages in some areas and excess housing in other areas. The regionalized nature of the problem helps to explain the broader lack of national focus on the issue. Geographic inequality refers to the differences in economic conditions, mobility, and growth in different parts of the country, or even between different communities within the same region or state. For instance, while 60 percent of Boston residents between 25 and 34 are college graduates, only 20 percent of the same age group in Lakeland, Florida, has achieved a similar level of education. Likewise, in the San Francisco Bay area, housing prices have risen so much faster than in the rest of the country that the higher wages offered to workers living or working in the region end up being consumed by higher land costs such that even high-income residents might spend over 30 percent of their income on housing. Meanwhile, economically depressed areas might offer cheaper housing, but also offer fewer prospects for local employment and access to amenities and services.[8]

A Problem Worth Addressing?

In 2018, Adem Bunkeddeko, who ran an unsuccessful campaign to challenge

Congresswoman Yvette Clarke in New York's 9th district, made affordable housing one of the key issues in his campaign. His campaign materials declared that Bunkeddeko considered affordable housing a "right" of citizenship and drew upon his experience as the child of Ugandan refugees who was raised in a one-bedroom apartment in Elmhurst, Queens, alongside his five siblings. When Bunkeddeko was growing up, affordable rents in Elmhurst enabled his father to continue his education as he worked to support the family. But the affordability of Elmhurst, like much of Queens, has changed. This situation, in Bunkeddeko's eyes, limits the potential of many Americans, not just those at the lowest end of the income spectrum, but individuals and families at many different levels who are paying too high a portion of their monthly income to afford to advance economically in other areas of their lives. "Housing is the central bedrock of the place from which people are able to start to live out their version of the American Dream," Bunkeddeko said to the *Nation*. "If you don't have a place to live, it's hard to imagine how you're going to be able to succeed."[9]

While Bunkeddeko wasn't successful in his bid to oust Clark, his approach to social welfare issues has become increasingly familiar among the younger generation of politicians and social activists. By contrast, many of the older generation of politicians are accustomed to, if not directly linked with, the patterns of real estate and broader economic development that have contributed to the current issue. While there are many potential solutions that have been debated by politicians and activists, any effective solution will most likely need to involve a significant shift in political attitudes.

Micah L. Issitt

Works Used

Covert, Bryce. "All of a Sudden, Politicians Are Ready to Tackle America's Housing Crisis." *The Nation*. Nov 20, 2018. Retrieved from https://www.thenation.com/article/affordable-housing-crisis-warren-booker-harris/.

Desilver, Drew. "For Most U.S. Workers, Real Wages Have Barely Budged in Decades." *Pew Research*. Aug 7, 2018. Retrieved from http://www.pewresearch.org/fact-tank/2018/08/07/for-most-us-workers-real-wages-have-barely-budged-for-decades/.

Furman, Jason. "Barriers to Shared Growth: The Case of Land Use Regulation and Economic Rents. *Obama White House*. Nov 20, 2015. Retrieved from https://obamawhitehouse.archives.gov/sites/default/files/page/files/20151120_barriers_shared_growth_land_use_regulation_and_economic_rents.pdf.

Hobbes, Michael. "America's Housing Crisis Is a Ticking Time Bomb." *Huffington Post*. June 19, 2018. Retrieved from https://www.huffingtonpost.com/entry/housing-crisis-inequality-harvard-report_us_5b27c1f1e4b056b2263c621e.

Schneider, Benjamin. "The American Housing Crisis Might Be Our Next Big Political Issue." *CityLab*. May 16, 2018. Retrieved from https://www.citylab.com/equity/2018/05/is-housing-americas-next-big-political-issue/560378/.

Shoag, Daniel. "Removing Barriers to Accessing High-Productivity Places." *The

Brookings Institution. Jan 31, 2019. Retrieved from https://www.brookings.edu/research/removing-barriers-to-accessing-high-productivity-places/.

"The Silent Crisis in America." *Home1*. Public Interest. 2018. Retrieved from http://home.one/about/#grve-scrolling-section-5c5b4da37e77b.

Sisson, Patrick. "The Housing Crisis Isn't Just about Affordability—It's about Economic Mobility, Too." *Curbed*. Vox Media. Apr 24, 2018. Retrieved from https://www.curbed.com/2018/4/24/17275068/jobs-mobility-high-rent-housing-costs.

Stevens, Glenn. "Affordable Housing: The Crisis No One Is Talking About." *NCHM*. National Center for Housing Management. Apr 8, 2016. Retrieved from http://www.nchm.org/Resources/Compliance-Corner/Review/ArticleId/140/Affordable-housing-the-crisis-no-one-is-talking-about.

Notes

1. Schneider, "The American Housing Crisis Might Be Our Next Big Political Issue."
2. Stevens, "Affordable Housing: The Crisis No One Is Talking About."
3. Desilver, "For Most U.S. Workers, Real Wages Have Barely Budged in Decades."
4. Hobbes, "America's Housing Crisis Is A Ticking Time Bomb."
5. "The Silent Crisis In America," *Home1*.
6. Sisson, "The Housing Crisis Isn't Just about Affordability—It's about Economic Mobility, Too."
7. Furman, "Barriers to Shared Growth: The Case of Land Use Regulation and Economic Rents."
8. Shoag, "Removing Barriers to Cccessing High-Productivity Places."
9. Covert, "All of a Sudden, Politicians Are Ready to Tackle America's Housing Crisis."

151 Years of America's Housing History

The Nation, May 24, 2018

1867: The first tenement-law regulation in America is enacted in New York City to ban the construction of rooms without ventilators and apartments without fire escapes.

1923: Under Mayor Daniel Hoan of the Socialist Party, Milwaukee completes construction of the country's first public-housing project.

1926: New York State passes the Limited Dividend Housing Companies Act, the first significant effort in the country to offer any kind of subsidy for affordable housing.

1934: The National Housing Act establishes the Federal Housing Administration, which insures mortgages for small, owner-occupied suburban homes as well as private multifamily housing.

1937: Congress passes the Housing Act of 1937. Originally intended to create public housing for poor and middle-income families, it is whittled down to apply only to low-income people.

1942: The Emergency Price Control Act establishes federal rent control for the first time. By January 1945, Scranton, Pennsylvania, is the only city of more than 100,000 residents with unregulated rents.

1944: The GI Bill provides mortgage-loan guarantees for home purchases by veterans.

1955: New York State introduces the Mitchell-Lama program, which subsidizes the construction of over 105,000 apartments for moderate- and middle-income residents.

1965: Congress establishes the Department of Housing and Urban Development (HUD) in a largely symbolic move to bring housing and slum-clearance programs to the cabinet level.

1968: Congress passes the Fair Housing Act, which outlaws discrimination in housing and in mortgage lending.

1973: The Nixon administration issues a moratorium on almost all subsidized-housing programs.

1974: The Housing and Community Development Act of 1974 establishes Section 8 housing programs as a replacement for public housing.

1976: The Supreme Court rules, in *Hills v. Gautreaux*, that the Chicago Housing Authority contributed to racial segregation in Chicago through discriminatory practices. HUD begins offering vouchers in the city to address poverty and segregation.

1982: Under Ronald Reagan, HUD's budget is slashed to under $40 billion, a decrease of more than 50 percent from 1976, when it was $83.6 billion.

1986: Reagan introduces the low-income housing tax credit, which remains the primary source of federal funding for low-cost housing today.

1992: Congress authorizes the HOPE VI urban-revitalization demonstration program to provide grants to support low-rise, mixed-income housing rather than high-rise public housing to address a severe lack of funding for repairs. Atlanta uses its funds to clear slums and construct mostly private housing, an approach copied by cities across the country.

2007: The housing market crashes. Nearly 3 million homes are foreclosed on in both 2009 and 2010.

1996: Bill Clinton announces the "one strike and you're out" initiative to evict public-housing tenants who have criminal convictions.

2005: HUD conducts its first official point-in-time count of homeless people in the country.

2007: The housing market crashes. Nearly 3 million homes are foreclosed on in both 2009 and 2010.

2012: The Obama administration creates the Rental Assistance Demonstration program, which authorizes the transformation of public housing into private-sector Section 8 housing.

2012: The Section 8 waiting lists stretch so long that nearly half of them are simply closed.

2018: HUD Secretary Ben Carson proposes raising the rent for tenants in subsidized housing as well as enabling public-housing authorities to impose work requirements.

Print Citations

CMS: "151 Years of America's Housing History." In *The Reference Shelf: Affordable Housing,* edited by Micah L. Issit, 9-11. Amenia, NY: Grey House Publishing, 2019.

MLA: "151 Years of America's Housing History." *The Reference Shelf: Affordable Housing,* edited by Micah L. Issit, Grey House Publishing, 2019, pp. 9-11.

APA: The Nation. (2019). 151 years of America's housing history. In Micah L. Issit (Ed.), *The reference shelf: Affordable housing* (pp. 9-11). Amenia, NY: Grey House Publishing.

A Brief Historical Overview of Affordable Rental Housing

National Low Income Housing Coalition, 2018

Affordable housing is a broad and complex subject intertwined with many disciplines: finance, economics, politics, and social services, to name a few. In spite of the complexity, advocates can come to an understanding of the essential workings of affordable housing and, in doing so, be prepared to advocate effectively for the programs and policies that can ensure access to decent, affordable housing for the people in need throughout their communities.

This article provides a broad, though not exhaustive, overview of the history of affordable rental housing programs in the United States and attempts to paint a picture of how those programs work together to meet the housing needs of low income people.

History

As with any federal program, federal housing programs grew and changed based on the economic, social, cultural, and political circumstances of the times. The programs and agencies that led to the federal department now known as HUD began in the early 1930s with construction and finance programs meant to alleviate some of the housing hardships caused by the Great Depression. An act of Congress in 1934 created the Federal Housing Administration, which made home ownership affordable for a broader segment of the public with the establishment of mortgage insurance programs. These programs made possible the low down payments and long-term mortgages that are commonplace today, but were almost unheard of at that time.

In 1937, the U.S. Housing Act sought to address the housing needs of low income people through public housing. The nation's housing stock at this time was of very poor quality in many parts of the country. Inadequate housing conditions such as the lack of hot running water or dilapidation were commonplace for poor families. Public housing was a significant improvement for those who had access to it. At the same time, the post-World War II migration from urban areas to the suburbs meant declining cities. Federal programs were developed to improve urban infrastructure and to clear "blight." This often meant wholesale destruction of neighborhoods and housing, albeit often low-quality housing, lived in by immigrants and people of color.

In 1965, Congress elevated housing to a cabinet-level agency of the federal government, creating HUD, which succeeded its predecessors, the National Housing Agency and the Housing and Home Finance Agency, respectively.

HUD is not the only federal agency to have begun housing programs in response to the problems of the Great Depression. The U.S. Department of Agriculture (USDA) sought to address the poor housing conditions of farmers and other rural people through the 1935 creation of the Resettlement Administration, a predecessor to USDA's Rural Development. USDA's rural rental and homeownership programs improved both housing access and housing quality for the rural poor.

The cost of operating public housing soon eclipsed the revenue brought in from resident rents, a reality endemic to any program that seeks to provide housing or other goods or services to people whose incomes are not great enough to afford the prices offered in the marketplace. In the 1960s, HUD began providing subsidies to public housing agencies (PHAs) that would help make up the difference between revenue from rents and the cost of adequately maintaining the housing. In 1969, Congress passed the "Brooke Amendment," codifying a limitation on the percentage of income a public housing resident could be expected to pay for rent. The original figure was 25% of income, and was later raised to the 30% standard that exists today. Advocates often refer to these as "Brooke rents," for Senator Edward W. Brooke, III (R-MA), for whom the amendment is named.

Beginning in the late 1950s and continuing into the 1960s, Congress created a number of programs that leveraged private investment to create new affordable rental housing. In general, these programs provided low interest rates or other subsidies to private owners who would purchase or rehabilitate housing to be rented at affordable rates. The growth in these private ownership programs resulted in a boom in affordable housing construction through the 1970s. However, once the contracts forged by HUD and private owners expired, or owners decided to pay their subsidized mortgages early, those affordable units could be lost from the stock.

The Civil Rights Acts of 1964 and 1968 included housing provisions that were intended to prevent discrimination against members of protected classes in private or public housing. Different presidential administrations have prioritized these fair housing provisions to varying extents, but their existence has provided leverage to advocates seeking to expand access to affordable, decent housing, particularly for people of color.

In January 1973, President Richard Nixon created a moratorium on the construction of new rental and homeownership housing by the major HUD programs. The following year, the Housing and Community Development Act of 1974 made significant changes to housing programs, marked by a focus on block grants and an increase in the authority granted to local jurisdictions (often referred to as "devolution of authority"). This act was the origin of the tenant-based and project-based Section 8 rental assistance programs, and it created the Community Development Block Grant (CDBG) from seven existing housing and infrastructure programs.

Structural changes in the American economy, deinstitutionalization of persons with mental illness, and a decline in housing and other support for low income people resulted in the dramatic increase in homelessness in the 1980s. The shock of visible homelessness spurred Congressional action, and the McKinney Act of 1987 (later renamed the McKinney-Vento Act) created new housing and social service programs within HUD specially designed to address homelessness.

Waves of private affordable housing owners deciding to "opt out" of the project-based Section 8 program occurred in the 1980s and 1990s. Housing advocates—including PHAs, nonprofit affordable housing developers, local government officials, nonprofit advocacy organizations and low income renters—organized to preserve this disappearing stock of affordable housing using whatever funding and financing was available to them.

The Department of the Treasury's Internal Revenue Service was given a role in affordable housing development in the Tax Reform Act of 1986 with the creation of the Low Income Housing Tax Credit, which provides tax credits to those investing in the development of affordable rental housing. That same act codified the use of private activity bonds for housing finance, authorizing the use of such bonds for the development of housing for homeownership, as well as the development of multi-family rental housing.

The Cranston-Gonzales National Affordable Housing Act of 1990 (NAHA) created the Comprehensive Affordable Housing Strategy (CHAS). It was now the obligation of jurisdictions to identify priority housing needs and to determine how to allocate the various block grants (such as CDBG) that they receive. CHAS is the statutory underpinning of the current Consolidated Plan obligation. Cranston-Gonzales also created the HOME program, which provides block grants to state and local governments for housing. In addition, NAHA created the Section 811 program, which has provided production and operating subsidies to nonprofits for housing persons with disabilities.

Housing advocates have worked for more than a decade for the establishment and funding of the national Housing Trust Fund (HTF), which is the first new housing resource in a generation. The HTF is highly targeted and is used to build, preserve, rehabilitate, and operate housing affordable to extremely low income people. HTF was signed into law by President George W. Bush in 2008 as a part of the Housing and Economic Recovery Act. In 2016, the first allocation of HTF dollars was provided to states.

Outside of the HTF, no significant investment in new housing affordable to the lowest income people has been made in more than 30 years, and there still exists a great shortage of housing affordable to that population. As studies from NLIHC show, the federal investment in housing has not increased at pace with the overall increase in the federal budget, and expenditures on housing go overwhelmingly to homeownership, not to rental housing for people with the greatest need. Federal spending caps, enacted in 2011, have only further strained efforts to adequately fund programs.

State and Local Housing Programs

State and local governments play a role in meeting the housing needs of their residents. The devolution of authority to local governments that began in the 1970s meant that local jurisdictions had greater responsibility for planning and carrying out

> **The majority of federal housing programs are appropriated, meaning that the funding amounts can change from year to year, or disappear altogether.**

housing programs. Some communities have responded to the decrease in federal housing resources by creating emergency and ongoing rental assistance programs, as well as housing production programs. These programs have been important to low income residents in the communities where they are available, but state and local efforts have not been enough to make up for the federal disinvestment in affordable housing.

Cities, counties, and states across the country have begun creating their own rental assistance programs as well as housing development programs, often called housing trust funds, to meet local housing needs and help fill in the gaps left by the decline in federal housing production and rental assistance. Local funding sources may be targeted to specific income groups, or may be created to meet the needs of a certain population, such as veterans, seniors, or families transitioning out of homelessness. Funding sources include local levy or bond measures and real estate transaction or document recording fees, among others.

Federal decision-making has had a direct impact on states' response to the shortage of housing affordable to extremely low income people. In 1999, the U.S. Supreme Court found in *Olmstead v. L.C.* that continued institutionalization of people with disabilities who were able to return to the community constituted discrimination under the Americans with Disabilities Act. This decision means that states are now developing and providing community-based permanent supportive housing for people with disabilities in response to *Olmstead* litigation, or in order to avoid future litigation.

Developing Affordable Housing at the Local Level

The expense of producing and operating housing affordable to low income renters, and the multitude of funding sources available to finance it, make affordable housing development a complicated task.

Affordable housing developers, including PHAs redeveloping their housing stock, must combine multiple sources of funding in order to finance housing development or preservation. These funding sources can be of federal, state, or local origin, and can also include private lending and grants or donations. Some developers include market-rate housing options within a development in order to generate revenue that will cross-subsidize units set aside for lower income tenants. Each funding source will have its own requirements for income or population targeting, as well as oversight requirements. Some funding sources require developers to meet certain environmental standards or other goals, such as historic preservation or transit-oriented development.

Accessing these many funding sources requires entry into application processes that may or may not have complementary timelines, and developers risk rejection of even the highest merit applications due to a shortage of resources. Developers incur costs before the first shovel hits the ground as they work to plan their developments around available funding sources and their associated requirements.

Developers encounter another set of requirements in the communities in which they work. They must operate according to local land use regulations, and can sometimes encounter community opposition to a planned development, which can jeopardize funder support for a project.

Once developments open, depending on the needs of the residents, services and supports may be included in the development. These can range from after-school programs to job training to physical or mental health care. This can mean working with another set of federal, state, and local programs, and nonprofit service providers.

In spite of these challenges, affordable housing developers succeed every day, building, rehabilitating, and preserving the quality housing low income people need at rents they can afford.

The Future of Affordable Housing

The need for affordable housing continues to grow, particularly the need for housing affordable to the lowest income people. Nationwide, there are only 35 units of housing affordable and available for every 100 extremely low income Americans. Federal housing assistance only serves one quarter of those who qualify for it. And special populations, such as disabled veterans returning from combat or lower income seniors, are increasing in number and need.

At the same time, the existing stock of affordable rental housing is disappearing due to deterioration and the exit of private owners from the affordable housing market. According to the National Housing Trust, our nation loses two affordable apartments each year for every one created. Local preservation efforts have seen success, and resources like the National Housing Preservation Database are helpful, but it is a race against time.

Finally, the very funding structure of most affordable housing programs puts them at risk, at both the federal and local levels. The majority of federal housing programs are appropriated, meaning that the funding amounts can change from year to year, or disappear altogether. State and local programs can be similarly volatile, because they are often dependent on revenue from fees or other market-driven sources, and are vulnerable to being swept into non-housing uses. Ensuring funding at amounts necessary to maintain programs at their current level of service, much less grow them, is a constant battle.

The Role of Advocates

Just as the Great Depression caused lawmakers to consider an expanded role for government in the provision and financing of housing, the Great Recession of 2008 and the ensuing slow recovery have inspired advocates, lawmakers, and the general public to take interest in the housing and other needs of lower income people, and to reconsider the role of government in housing, particularly in homeowner-owned housing.

Affordable housing advocates have a unique opportunity to make the case for affordable rental housing with members of Congress as well as with local policy-makers. As the articles in this Guide demonstrate, subsidized rental housing is more cost effective and sustainable than the alternative, be it institutionalization, home-lessness, or grinding hardship for working poor families. And after decades of a clear over-investment in homeownership, the housing market collapse, and the growth of a gaping divide between the resources and future prospects of the highest and low-est income people, it is clearly time for federal housing policy to be rebalanced in favor of addressing the greatest housing needs.

Those who wish to see an end to homelessness must be unyielding in their ad-vocacy for rental housing that is affordable to the lowest income people. Over the eight decades of direct federal involvement in housing, we have learned much about how the government, private, and public sectors can partner with communities to create the affordable housing that will improve lives and heal whole neighborhoods. We must take this evidence, and our stories, to lawmakers to show them that this can, and must, be done.

For More Information

HUD Historical Background, http://1.usa. gov/11P11P2

NLIHC's *Changing Priorities: The Federal Government and Housing Assistance, 1976-2007*, http://nlihc.org/sites/default/files/Changing-Priorities-Report_August-2002.pdf

NLIHC's *Affordable Housing is Nowhere to be Found for Millions*, http://nlihc.org/sites/default/files/Housing-Spotlight_Volume-5_Issue-1.pdf

National Housing Trust Fund, www.nhtf.org

The Housing Trust Fund Project of the Center for Community Change, http://housingtrustfundproject.org/

National Housing Preservation Database http://www.preservationdatabase.org/

Print Citations

CMS: "A Brief Historical Overview of Affordable Rental Housing." In *The Reference Shelf: Affordable Housing*, edited by Micah L. Issit, 12-17. Amenia, NY: Grey House Publishing, 2019.

MLA: "A Brief Historical Overview of Affordable Rental Housing." *The Reference Shelf: Affordable Housing*, edited by Micah L. Issit, Grey House Publishing, 2019, pp. 12-17.

APA: National Low Income Housing Coalition. (2019). A brief historical overview of afford-able rental housing. In Micah L. Issit (Ed.), *The reference shelf: Affordable housing* (pp. 12-17). Amenia, NY: Grey House Publishing.

The Causes and Costs of the Worst Crisis Since the Great Depression

By Kimberly Amadeo
The Balance, November 7, 2018

The 2008 financial crisis is the worst economic disaster since the Great Depression of 1929. It occurred despite Federal Reserve and Treasury Department efforts to prevent it.

It led to the Great Recession. That's when housing prices fell 31.8 percent, more than the price plunge during the Depression. Two years after the recession ended, unemployment was still above 9 percent. That's not counting discouraged workers who had given up looking for work.

Causes

The first sign that the economy was in trouble occurred in 2006. That's when housing prices started to fall. At first, realtors applauded. They thought the overheated housing market would return to a more sustainable level.

Realtors didn't realize there were too many homeowners with questionable credit. Banks had allowed people to take out loans for 100 percent or more of the value of their new homes. Many blamed the Community Reinvestment Act. It pushed banks to make investments in subprime areas, but that wasn't the underlying cause.

The Gramm-Rudman Act was the real villain. It allowed banks to engage in trading profitable derivatives that they sold to investors. These mortgage-backed securities needed home loans as collateral. The derivatives created an insatiable demand for more and more mortgages.

Hedge funds and other financial institutions around the world owned the mortgage-backed securities. The securities were also in mutual funds, corporate assets, and pension funds. The banks had chopped up the original mortgages and resold them in tranches. That made the derivatives impossible to price.

Why did stodgy pension funds buy such risky assets? They thought an insurance product called credit default swaps protected them. A traditional insurance company known as the American International Group sold these swaps. When the derivatives lost value, AIG didn't have enough cash flow to honor all the swaps.

The first signs of the financial crisis appeared in 2007. Banks panicked when they realized they would have to absorb the losses. They stopped lending to each

---

other. They didn't want other banks giving them worthless mortgages as collateral. No one wanted to get stuck holding the bag. As a result, interbank borrowing costs, called Libor, rose. This mistrust within the banking community was the primary cause of the 2008 financial crisis.

The Federal Reserve began pumping liquidity into the banking system via the Term Auction Facility. But that wasn't enough.

Costs

The 2008 financial crisis timeline began in March 2008. Investors sold off their shares of investment bank Bear Stearns because it had too many of the toxic assets. Bear approached JP Morgan Chase to bail it out. The Fed had to sweeten the deal with a **$30 billion** guarantee. By 2012, the Fed had received full payment for its loan.

After the Bear Stearns bailout, Wall Street thought the panic was over. Instead, the situation deteriorated throughout the summer of 2008.

Congress authorized the Treasury Secretary to take over mortgage companies Fannie Mae and Freddie Mac. It cost **$187 billion** at the time. Since then, Treasury has made enough in profits to pay off the cost.

On September 16, 2008, the Fed loaned $85 billion to AIG as a bailout. In October and November, the Fed and Treasury restructured the bailout. The total cost ballooned to **$182 billion**. But by 2012, the government made a $22.7 billion profit when Treasury sold its last AIG shares. The value of the company had risen that much in four years.

On September 17, 2008, the crisis created a run on money market funds. Companies park excess cash there to earn interest on it overnight. Banks then use those funds to make short-term loans. During the run, companies moved a record $144.5 billion out of their money market accounts into even safer

> **The Great Recession—that's when housing prices fell 31.8 percent, more than the price plunge during the Depression.**

Treasury bonds. If these accounts had gone bankrupt, business activities and the economy would have ground to a halt.

That crisis called for a massive government intervention. Three days later, Treasury Secretary Henry Paulson and Fed Chair Ben Bernanke submitted a $700 billion bailout package to Congress. Their fast response stopped the run. But Republicans blocked the bill for two weeks. They didn't want to bail out banks. They only approved the bill after global stock markets almost collapsed.

The bailout package never cost the taxpayer the full $700 billion. Treasury disbursed **$439.6 billion** from the Troubled Asset Relief Program. By 2018, it had put $442.6 billion back into the fund. It made $3 billion in profit. How did it do this? It bought shares of the companies it bailed out when prices were low. It wisely sold them when prices were high.

The TARP funds helped five areas. Treasury used $245.1 billion to buy bank preferred stocks as a way to give them cash. Another $80.7 billion bailed out auto companies. It contributed $67.8 billion to the $182 billion bailout of insurance company AIG. Another $19.1 billion went to shore up credit markets. The bank repaid $23.6 billion, creating a $4.5 billion profit. The Homeowner Affordability and Stability Plan disbursed $27.9 billion to modify mortgages.

President Obama didn't use the remaining $700 billion allocated for TARP. He didn't want to bail out any more businesses. Instead, he asked Congress for an economic stimulus package. On February 17, 2009, he signed the American Recovery and Reinvestment Act. It had tax cuts, stimulus checks, and public works spending. By 2011, it put **$831 billion** directly into the the pockets of consumers and small businesses. It was enough to end the financial crisis by July 2009.

How It Could Happen Again

Many legislators blame Fannie and Freddie for the entire crisis. To them, the solution is to close or privatize the two agencies. But if they were shut down, the housing market would collapse. They guarantee 90 percent of all mortgages. Furthermore, securitization, or the bundling and reselling of loans, has spread to more than just housing.

The government must step in to regulate. Congress passed the Dodd-Frank Wall Street Reform Act to prevent banks from taking on too much risk. It allows the Fed to reduce bank size for those that become too big to fail.

But it left many of the measures up to federal regulators to sort out the details. Meanwhile, banks keep getting bigger and are pushing to get rid of even this regulation. The financial crisis of 2008 proved that banks could not regulate themselves. Without government oversight like Dodd-Frank, they could create another global crisis.

NOTE: The Federal Reserve believed the subprime mortgage crisis would remain confined to the housing sector. Fed officials didn't know how far the damage would spread. They didn't understand the actual causes of the subprime mortgage crisis until later.

Print Citations

CMS: Amadeo, Kimberly. "The Causes and Costs of the Worst Crisis Since the Great Depression." In *The Reference Shelf: Affordable Housing*, edited by Micah L. Issit, 18-20. Amenia, NY: Grey House Publishing, 2019.

MLA: Amadeo, Kimberly. "The Causes and Costs of the Worst Crisis Since the Great Depression." *The Reference Shelf: Affordable Housing*, edited by Micah L. Issit, Grey House Publishing, 2019, pp. 18-20.

APA: Amadeo, K. (2019). The causes and costs of the worst crisis since the Great Depression. In Micah L. Issit (Ed.), *The reference shelf: Affordable housing* (pp.18-20). Amenia, NY: Grey House Publishing.

The Forgotten History of the Financial Crisis

By Adam Tooze
Foreign Affairs, September/October 2018

"September and October of 2008 was the worst financial crisis in global history, including the Great Depression." Ben Bernanke, then the chair of the U.S. Federal Reserve, made this remarkable claim in November 2009, just one year after the meltdown. Looking back today, a decade after the crisis, there is every reason to agree with Bernanke's assessment: 2008 should serve as a warning of the scale and speed with which global financial crises can unfold in the twenty-first century.

The basic story of the financial crisis is familiar enough. The trouble began in 2007 with a downturn in U.S. and European real estate markets; as housing prices plunged from California to Ireland, homeowners fell behind on their mortgage payments, and lenders soon began to feel the heat. Thanks to the deep integration of global banking, securities, and funding markets, the contagion quickly spread to major financial institutions around the world. By late 2008, banks in Belgium, France, Germany, Ireland, Latvia, the Netherlands, Portugal, Russia, Spain, South Korea, the United Kingdom, and the United States were all facing existential crises. Many had already collapsed, and many others would before long.

The Great Depression of the 1930s is remembered as the worst economic disaster in modern history—one that resulted in large part from inept policy responses—but it was far less synchronized than the crash in 2008. Although more banks failed during the Depression, these failures were scattered between 1929 and 1933 and involved far smaller balance sheets. In 2008, both the scale and the speed of the implosion were breathtaking. According to data from the Bank for International Settlements, gross capital flows around the world plunged by 90 percent between 2007 and 2008.

As capital flows dried up, the crisis soon morphed into a crushing recession in the real economy. The "great trade collapse" of 2008 was the most severe synchronized contraction in international trade ever recorded. Within nine months of their pre-crisis peak, in April 2008, global exports were down by 22 percent. (During the Great Depression, it took nearly two years for trade to slump by a similar amount.) In the United States between late 2008 and early 2009, 800,000 people were losing their jobs every month. By 2015, over nine million American families would lose their homes to foreclosure—the largest forced population movement in the United

States since the Dust Bowl. In Europe, meanwhile, failing banks and fragile public finances created a crisis that nearly split the eurozone.

Ten years later, there is little consensus about the meaning of 2008 and its aftermath. Partial narratives have emerged to highlight this or that aspect of the crisis, even as crucial elements of the story have been forgotten. In the United States, memories have centered on the government recklessness and private criminality that led up to the crash; in Europe, leaders have been content to blame everything on the Americans.

In fact, bankers on both sides of the Atlantic created the system that imploded in 2008. The collapse could easily have devastated both the U.S. and the European economies had it not been for improvisation on the part of U.S. officials at the Federal Reserve, who leveraged trans-atlantic connections they had inherited from the twentieth century to stop the global bank run. That this reality has been obscured speaks both to the contentious politics of managing global finances and to the growing distance between the United States and Europe. More important, it forces a question about the future of financial globalization: How will a multipolar world that has moved beyond the transatlantic structures of the last century cope with the next crisis?

Tall Tales

One of the more common tropes to emerge since 2008 is that no one predicted the crisis. This is an after-the-fact construction. In truth, there were many predictions of a crisis—just not of the crisis that ultimately arrived.

Macroeconomists around the world had long warned of global imbalances stemming from U.S. trade and budget deficits and China's accumulation of U.S. debt, which they feared could trigger a global dollar selloff. The economist Paul Krugman warned in 2006 of "a Wile E. Coyote moment," in which investors, recognizing the poor fundamentals of the U.S. economy, would suddenly flee dollar-denominated assets, crippling the world economy and sending interest rates sky-high.

But the best and the brightest were reading the wrong signs. When the crisis came, the Chinese did not sell off U.S. assets. Although they reduced their holdings in U.S.-government-sponsored enterprises such as the mortgage lenders Fannie Mae and Freddie Mac, they increased their purchases of U.S. Treasury bonds, refusing to join the Russians in a bear raid on the dollar. Rather than falling as predicted, the dollar actually rose in the fall of 2008. What U.S. authorities were facing was not a Sino-American meltdown but an implosion of the transatlantic banking system, a crisis of financial capitalism.

And the crisis was general, not just American, although the Europeans had a hard time believing it. When, over the weekend of September 13–14, 2008, U.S. Treasury Secretary Henry Paulson and other officials tried to arrange the sale of the failed investment bank Lehman Brothers to the British bank Barclays, the reaction of Alistair Darling, the British chancellor of the exchequer, was telling. He did not want, he told his American counterparts, to "import" the United States' "cancer"—this despite the fact that the United Kingdom's own banks were already tumbling around him.

The French and the Germans were no less emphatic. In September 2008, as the crisis was going global, the German finance minister, Peer Steinbrück, declared that it was "an American problem" that would cause the United States to "lose its status as the superpower of the world financial system." French President Nicolas Sarkozy announced that U.S.-style "laissez faire" was "finished." To Europeans, the idea of an American crisis made sense. The United States had allowed itself to be sucked into misguided wars of choice while refusing to pay for them. It was living far beyond its means, and the crisis was its comeuppance. But confident predictions that this was a U.S. problem were quickly overtaken by events. Not only were Europe's banks deeply involved in the U.S. subprime crisis, but their business models left them desperately dependent on dollar funding. The result was to send the continent into an economic and political crisis from which it is only now recovering.

Even today, Americans and Europeans have very different memories of the financial crisis. For many American commentators, it stands as a moment in a protracted arc of national decline and the prehistory of the radicalization of the Republican Party. In September 2008, the Republican-led House of Representatives voted against the Bush administration's bailout plan to save the national economy from imminent implosion (although it passed a similar bill in early October); a few months later, after a lost election and at a time when 800,000 Americans were being thrown out of work every month, House Republicans voted nearly unanimously against President Barack Obama's stimulus bill. The crisis ushered in a new era of absolute partisan antagonism that would rock American democracy to its foundations.

> **According to data from the Bank for International Settlements, gross capital flows around the world plunged by 90 percent between 2007 and 2008.**

Europeans, meanwhile, remain content to let the United States shoulder the blame. France and Germany have no equivalent of *The Big Short*—the best-selling book (and later movie) that dramatized the events of 2008 as an all-American conflict between the forces of herd instinct and rugged individualism, embodied by the heterodox speculators who saw the crisis coming. Germans cannot ignore that Deutsche Bank was a major player in those events, but they can easily explain this away by claiming that the bank abandoned its German soul. And just as the Europeans have chosen to forget their own mistakes, so, too, have they forgotten what the crisis revealed about Europe's dependence on the United States—an inconvenient truth for European elites at a time when Brussels and Washington are drifting apart.

Print Citations

CMS: Tooze, Adam. "The Forgotten History of the Financial Crisis." In *The Reference Shelf: Affordable Housing,* edited by Micah L. Issit, 21-24. Amenia, NY: Grey House Publishing, 2019.

MLA: Tooze, Adam. "The Forgotten History of the Financial Crisis." *The Reference Shelf: Affordable Housing,* edited by Micah L. Issit, Grey House Publishing, 2019, pp. 21-24.

APA: Tooze, A. (2019). The forgotten history of the financial crisis. In Micah L. Issit (Ed.), *The reference shelf: Affordable housing* (pp. 21-24). Amenia, NY: Grey House Publishing.

The Deep, Uniquely American Roots of Our Affordable-Housing Crisis

By Bryce Covert
The Nation, May 24, 2018

When Rosalina Hernández and her husband moved into their studio apartment on Los Angeles Street in South Central LA 15 years ago, the place was just for the two of them and the baby they were expecting. Back then, it wasn't too hard to find what they needed: an apartment they could afford with just a bit more space.

But as their family grew, they remained stuck in place. Eventually, six people—Rosalina, her husband, and their four children—were sharing the one main room, a small kitchen, and a bathroom. Today, the tidy living room is also the dining room and bedroom; the bathroom serves as a makeshift closet. "It is hard, because we're six," Rosalina says in Spanish, clasping her hands in her lap. "It's too small for six." When her oldest son, now a freshman in college, needed to concentrate on schoolwork, he'd lock himself in the bathroom until the early-morning hours.

Her children ask her why they can't have their own rooms. Her second-oldest son has always had a particular dream: to have a house, a dog, and a tree. "I would have liked to," Rosalina says haltingly, wiping away the tears. They've looked for a bigger place, but they just can't afford it. "We have to choose between [paying more] rent [for] a bigger space, or giving [our children] food and shoes." They currently pay $700 a month in rent, something that Rosalina and her husband can afford on his salary as a garment worker. A three-bedroom apartment in LA easily goes for more than triple that. Soon, though, the Hernándezes will have no choice: All of the residents in their building are being evicted. The owner has decided to sell it, and a developer plans to raze it and build a new complex in its place. Many families have already left, plywood nailed over their doors to mark their departure. The Hernándezes were able to get a year's extension because their youngest daughter has a severe learning disability, but the grace period ends next May.

The uncertainty has taken its toll. Rosalina's 4-year-old daughter asks her, "Mommy, am I still going to have my same friends? Mommy, am I going to have my same teacher?" If she could, Rosalina would keep her family in that same small apartment—at least it's home. "*Cuatros paredes tienen historia*," she says. Four walls have a history.

Among American cities, Los Angeles is second only to Las Vegas (and tied with Orlando, Florida) in having the severest shortage of affordable housing for its poorest renters, with just 17 homes for every 100 extremely low-income families. The median rent for a one-bedroom apartment is nearly $1,400 a month, making it one of the most unaffordable markets in the country. Over half of the renters in LA are paying more than 30 percent of their income in rent, above what's considered affordable; for nearly a third of those residents, rent eats up more than half of their income. "It's not a housing crisis," says Larry Gross, executive director of the grassroots group Coalition for Economic Survival. "It's a housing catastrophe."

When rents are that high, those people lucky enough to find a place have to make other difficult choices. "They have to sacrifice health care, food, clothing for their children, education, transport—all the basic necessities," says Dagan R. Bayliss, director of organizing at Strategic Actions for a Just Economy, which is working with Rosalina and her family. Many families have two or even three people living in a single room to bring down costs. More than half of the most heavily crowded areas in the country, where the homes have more than one person per room, are located in Los Angeles and Orange counties, according to US Census data spanning from 2008 to 2012.

Other people decide to move where rents are cheaper, but that often means longer commutes and higher transportation costs, not to mention leaving behind family or a familiar community. The Hernándezes have considered it. Rosalina's sister and brother-in-law went to San Bernardino, where the rents are much lower, but her husband would have to drive more than an hour into the city for work every day. He currently walks to his job, and Rosalina can walk to her children's schools, so they don't need a car. If they moved, they'd have to shoulder that extra expense and travel time. Still, many working people make that trade-off. "We're becoming a tale of two cities: the very rich, and the very low-income who are on some type of subsidies," Gross says. "The middle class, the working class, are being pushed out."

But if LA is the extreme, it is also a harbinger of trends that are under way everywhere in a country in which rents are increasing while incomes stagnate. There is nowhere in the United States that a family like the Hernándezes can easily find an affordable and adequate place to live. Nationwide, there are just 35 affordable and available rental homes for every 100 extremely low-income families—those who either live in poverty or earn less than 30 percent of the median income in their area. It's a problem in every major city and in every state. Nationally, nearly half of renters spend more than 30 percent of their income on housing.

It may feel as though the country has always failed to offer an affordable home to everyone who needs one. But in 1960, only about a quarter of renters spent more than 30 percent of their income on housing. In 1970, a 300,000-unit surplus of affordable rental homes meant that nearly every American could find a place to live. "When there was an adequate supply of housing for low-income people, we did not have widespread homelessness in this country," says Nan Roman, president of the National Alliance to End Homelessness. At the time, "the word 'homelessness' was relatively unknown," says the Rev. David Bloom, a longtime advocate for the homeless, who adds that when he first used a word processor in the early 1980s, the spell-check didn't even recognize the word. Today, there's a deficit of more than 7.2

million rental homes inexpensive enough for the lowest-income people to afford, and nearly 554,000 Americans are homeless on any given night.

How did we get here? The mismatch between the number of people needing homes and the amount of affordable housing available isn't unique to this moment in history, or even to the United States. Matthew G. Lasner, associate professor at Hunter College's Urban Policy and Planning Department, describes housing shortages as a "product of industrial capitalism. The minute we see people flooding in from the countryside in search of work to cities, we see housing inequality emerging." As their populations became urbanized, countries like Britain and Germany started to experiment with government subsidies for housing around the time of the First World War, ultimately developing programs that provided housing for many people, not just for the poorest. But despite the efforts of Progressive Era reformers, the idea failed to take root in the United States. "We were giving

> **Nationwide, there are just 35 affordable and available rental homes for every 100 extremely low-income families.**

land away for free out west," Lasner notes, but "the idea of the government actually helping the [urban] poor, at a time when one of the prevailing ideas about poverty was [that] it was a moral failure, was beyond the pale of political discourse." Today's crisis can be traced back to those early beliefs about poverty and private property. The federal government never developed a national plan to coordinate the construction of affordable housing where it was needed or required any city to construct it, and it never successfully challenged the notion that housing was a commodity, not a right.

The catastrophe of the Great Depression, which led to nearly 13 million unemployed and hundreds of homeless encampments across the country, shifted the political calculus in Washington. For a brief period of time, a different approach to housing—and a completely different way of thinking about poverty—seemed possible. From 1933 to 1941, President Franklin Roosevelt launched a range of employment programs, including the Public Works Administration, which he tasked with building model homes, among other major construction projects, thus addressing the twin crises of unemployment and unaffordable housing. PWA-built homes, which housed both the poor and the middle class, were often attractive, equipped with laundry facilities, meeting rooms, playgrounds, even libraries.

Yet the PWA wasn't a comprehensive housing program, and it provided housing only for a small share of Americans. It also inaugurated the long history of racial segregation in public housing, as most of the PWA-built developments were either divided by race or open only to whites. But the PWA's housing initiatives were significant enough that the real-estate industry, which realized it had a growing competitor, fought back. Members of the National Association of Real Estate Boards—today known as the National Association of Realtors—took to publishing columns in the *Saturday Evening Post* railing against the New Deal housing program as communistic.

Meanwhile, social reformers and their allies in Congress, like Senator Robert Wagner, were pushing for a true federal housing program—one that "must not be confined to demonstration projects, or to the improvement of conditions in limited though well-selected areas," Wagner declared in a speech in 1936. "It must encompass the basic housing need of the population as a whole." Their solution was a bill that became the Housing Act of 1937, which, when first drafted, reflected an entirely new way of thinking about housing in the United States. It would have provided public housing for both the poor and the middle class, as well as give the federal government more power to determine where that housing would be built. But over years of debate—Wagner introduced housing bills in each of the three years leading up to 1937—the legislation's most radical pieces were hollowed out. The National Association of Real Estate Boards proved to be a powerful enemy of high-quality, widely accessible public housing, and succeeded in profoundly weakening the bill. Ultimately, the 1937 law provided housing only for the poor and allowed communities to opt out of constructing any affordable housing at all. It included low cost ceilings, which meant that public housing couldn't become too desirable, as well as eligibility criteria that prevented the middle class from qualifying for it. Southern Democrats ensured that the housing could be racially segregated. Perhaps most counterproductive, the legislation included a requirement forcing public-housing authorities to demolish one unit of substandard housing for every new one built, raising costs and keeping the supply capped. "If it had been the bill that housing experts had imagined," Lasner says, "we would be facing a very different housing landscape today."

The public housing built thereafter was in line with what we think of today: housing projects for the poorest, cheaply built and concentrated far from the communities that refused to accept them. Though public housing still supplies more than 2 million people with permanently affordable homes, it provides housing for only a fraction of the 40 million Americans in poverty, and it leaves the private housing market almost entirely intact.

The legacy of the 1937 law is clearly seen in Los Angeles today. There are just 14 public-housing facilities, with just over 6,500 units, in a city of about 4 million people, an estimated 21.5 percent of whom live in poverty. In the 1950s, the City Council sank a plan to build 10,000 units of public housing using $100 million from the federal government. Around the same time, California voters approved a referendum requiring city or county approval for public-housing site selection, hamstringing development. For its part, New York City runs 326 facilities—23 times as many as LA—though it has double the population and a lower poverty rate. "Even though we've had all these liberal mayors," says Gary Blasi, a law professor emeritus at UCLA, "there's still virtually no coordinated or strategic policy to increase the amount of affordable housing."

Subsequent federal efforts fell prey to the same forces that undermined the 1937 bill. The Housing Act of 1949 aimed to provide "a decent home and suitable living environment for every American family," and resulted in the construction of nearly 324,000 units over ten years, but Congress failed to appropriate adequate funding. Southern Democrats, joined by some of their Northern counterparts, again prevented the law from prohibiting segregation.

Congress's failure to allocate sufficient funds for public housing would, over the ensuing decades, lead to the long-term neglect of public-housing projects. As a result, many were demolished. Starting in 1972, the Department of Housing and Urban Development (HUD) doled out grants that cities used to tear down abandoned or dilapidated housing. The country has lost 250,000 public-housing units since the mid-1990s alone.

In 1973, citing "mounting evidence of basic defects in some of our housing programs," the Nixon administration issued a moratorium on nearly all subsidized-housing programs. The symbolism was clear: During congressional hearings on the move, Senator William Proxmire declared, "The historic pledge of a decent home in a suitable environment for all Americans has been abandoned." A year later, Congress authorized a new approach to housing the poor: the Section 8 program, which provides poor people with vouchers that they can spend on private housing. Yet obtaining housing with a voucher in the private market can be fraught with challenges; not only are there few affordable units, but in many parts of the country, it is legal for landlords to reject voucher-holders. If a voucher recipient can't find a home within 60 or 90 days, she loses her subsidy. And as with public housing, Congress has never given Section 8 enough funds to meet the demand: Today, just one in four families who are eligible for federal rental assistance actually gets it. Meanwhile, moderate-income families who can't afford housing don't qualify.

And things only got worse. When Ronald Reagan assumed the presidency, public housing became one of the biggest targets of his anti-government, pro-market worldview. With Reagan in the White House, HUD's budget was cut by more than half, falling from $83.6 billion in 1976 to less than $40 billion by 1982; it has never recovered. Federal spending on housing assistance hemorrhaged by 50 percent during the same period. Homelessness, in his administration's view, was a personal failing; homeless people were homeless "by choice," Reagan said on *Good Morning America* in 1984.

Like Nixon, Reagan combined cuts to public housing with a housing program that expanded the role of the private sector. In his landmark 1986 tax package, he included a measure that is still the main source of federal funding for affordable housing today: the low-income housing tax credit (LIHTC). Developers gain access to the credit by pledging to build affordable housing. But the housing they build usually doesn't reach the poorest families, and it requires securing complicated funding sources, which prolongs construction time. Plus "developers would almost always prefer to build more [LIHTC] housing in low-income, segregated neighborhoods," says Richard Rothstein, author of *The Color of Law*. "The land is cheaper there, and they don't have to hold 100 community meetings to explain why they're putting poor people in their precious community."

Decades after Nixon and Reagan, these two market-based solutions—tax credits to get developers to build low-cost units, and vouchers that supposedly help poor people afford them—provide the dominant share of affordable housing. Leaders and lawmakers, including Democratic presidents, have by and large failed to challenge this status quo. Bill Clinton, who failed to increase HUD's budget and even let it decline for most of his tenure, once declared, "Public housing has never been a right; it has always been a privilege."

As the federal government disinvested, other cheap housing vanished too. From 1970 to the mid-1980s, 1 million single-room-occupancy (SRO) apartments—modest units that people could rent by the day or week—disappeared as cities cleared them out and developers tore the buildings down to build commercial properties or luxury housing. Multifamily housing was converted into co-ops and condominiums. Some of these homes hadn't been decent places to live, but the former residents weren't given a replacement. "A lot of times, when we improve things, we don't improve them for the people who are living there," says Nan Roman. "We improve them for someone else to live there."

Between 1995 and 2016, Los Angeles lost more than 5,400 federally subsidized housing units, and the production of affordable housing has stagnated, too. Meanwhile, market-rate development boomed. "Luxury-market rate—that's the only category in which we've come close to our production goals," says Becky Dennison, executive director of Venice Community Housing. In 2015, over 80 percent of new apartments were luxury units.

Los Angeles's Skid Row, 52 blocks where the city has corralled both its homeless services and homeless population, is the logical result when a housing market in a booming city is left to its own devices. Past the shiny skyscrapers of New Downtown and the hipster cafes of Little Tokyo, the sidewalks are filled with tents, shopping carts, folding chairs, pots, pans, and the other bits and pieces of people's lives. The tents that line almost every inch of the sidewalk are makeshift homes, connected to one another with ropes, tarps, poles, and umbrellas. The air hums with quarrels and boom-box music and smells of bodies and trash. Skid Row has been described as a refugee camp for Americans—and in its appearance and purpose, that's exactly what it is.

Jojo Smith lived in a tent on San Pedro Street for six years starting in 2006. He tried to get into a housing program but was always told that the waiting lists were full. For those six years, Smith was woken up in the early hours of the morning every day by the police and told to pack up his stuff and move along, only to have to set everything back up that evening. The wake-up calls are less regular today, but they still make people's lives chaotic. There are few water fountains or public bathrooms, let alone showers or laundry facilities. The scant trash cans fill up quickly and are rarely emptied by the city. "It shows you that the city is not caring about people," Smith says. "Homeless people are humans too."

Most of those living in tents would prefer four solid walls. "They're constantly saying that folks are resisting services. No, people are resisting shelters because of the simple fact that it's not your own home," Smith says. "They want housing." Shelters come with a maze of rules and regulations to navigate, including bans on pets and couples living together. Some people with mental-health issues struggle to sleep in the crowded rooms.

At the last official count, there were nearly 60,000 homeless people in Los Angeles County on any given night in 2017, up 23 percent from the year before, although that's likely still an undercount. About three-quarters of these people are unsheltered, living in tents or cars. Even as the city moves more people into housing, many others are getting pushed out of it and into homelessness. "Too many poor people and not enough housing means some people will get left out," Blasi notes. Anything that makes a poor person less able to compete for housing—mental illness, a disability, or just being black and a victim of discrimination—makes them more likely to fall into homelessness.

LA's laissez-faire approach to housing shows up in the factors driving its swelling homeless population. The city does little to prevent affordable housing from being demolished. Gross's organization estimates that 23,550 units of affordable housing have been lost thanks to a law that allows landlords to evict tenants when they decide to demolish or sell their buildings—exactly the circumstances that the Hernández family now faces. LA also has few robust rent-control laws, which played a role in rents rising 20 percent between 1990 and 2009, even as incomes dropped.

And decades of failing to construct new affordable units have resulted in a situation in which the demand for single-room apartments is so acute that there is virtually nothing available. Zoning restrictions and local opposition, which were given outsize political power in the 1940s and '50s, make it virtually impossible to build more housing in the city. "There is really powerful NIMBYism," Blasi says. "Anywhere middle-class people get a toehold, they're pulling up the ladders as quick as they can."

In the 1990s, the national crisis in affordable housing didn't feel as acute because income growth was relatively strong, giving people more of a cushion to afford their rent. But when the subprime-mortgage crisis hit in 2007, America's long-term refusal to deal with housing was once again laid bare. If modern mass homelessness began in the 1980s, the foreclosure and housing crises at the end of the 2000s represented a second wave that redoubled the problem. Nearly 3 million homes were foreclosed on in both 2009 and 2010; those homeowners sank back into the rental market, competing for cheap units with the low-income people who were already renting. Millennials delayed homeownership. The share of households renting in the country's 50 largest cities climbed from 36 percent in 2006 to over 40 percent in 2014. Roughly 10 million more families rented in 2016 compared with the decade prior. The vacancy rate for rental units has fallen since the end of the recession and is lower today than it was in 1986. "The supply is just not keeping up," says Diane Yentel, president of the National Low Income Housing Coalition. "That is leading, in many communities, to skyrocketing rents, [which are] felt most severely amongst the lowest-income people." There's been a 32 percent rise in the median asking rent since 2000, and the number of households that are rent-burdened, or forced to spend more than 30 percent of their income on rent, increased 19 percent between 2001 and 2015.

The financial crisis meant that Ericka Newsome didn't get a raise in January 2009, yet the rent on her studio apartment in her hometown of Pasadena, just northeast of downtown LA, went up. Newsome had been hired as a teller by a bank in 2005 and was promoted soon after. For the first time, she was living in her own place. But by March 2009, she was living in her car. Her boss eventually found out, and she lost her job in June over concerns that customers would see her sleeping in her vehicle.

"I didn't know where to go or where to turn," Newsome says. She couldn't afford a new apartment without a job, and she couldn't find a shelter with an available space. She lived briefly with a childhood friend in 2010, working during that time to earn her certification as a pharmacy technician. But she couldn't find a job in the midst of the recession. She struggled with mental-health issues. Eventually, her friend asked her to leave, and she had to give up her car.

Newsome found her way to Skid Row in 2016. She still remembers her first night there: She tried to find a spot that felt safe where she could sleep for the night, but as a solitary woman, she attracted men's attention. So she chose an isolated spot to set up camp. "The first night was scary," she recalls. "I had to stay up all night for my safety." Newsome spent her days sleeping or walking through the streets and riding the trains. An outreach team eventually helped her get into temporary housing and then an SRO, but both felt unsafe and unsanitary. Finally, she had a stroke of luck: Newsome was approved for a housing voucher, and an organization called Brilliant Corners connected her with a case manager who helped her look for an apartment. That help was needed: Although she found a number of apartments close to Pasadena that she really liked, landlords repeatedly told her that they wouldn't accept her housing voucher. She also suspects that she was being discriminated against because she was black. "It was like, immediately I was getting labeled as a person who is not safe to live in their building or be part of their neighborhood," she says.

Newsome looked for a place for nearly a year. Finally, with her case manager making calls on her behalf, she found an efficiency studio in Highland Park, close to Pasadena, in April of last year. When the landlord accepted her application, "it was such a happy moment for me," she recalls, a broad smile transforming her face. "Since then, things became easier. I was able to focus on my mental health…because I had a safe place to go home to." She began the pharmacy-technician recertification process and is also working toward becoming a personal trainer. "It's like a second chance for me to change my life and get myself more independent, more financially stable, and actually have a good, strong career job," she says. Eventually, she wants to leave the voucher program altogether. "I want to be able to say, 'This is my place.'"

The housing crisis "is like a game of musical chairs," says Nan Roman. "There's just not enough chairs for the number of people." And the private sector simply can't solve this problem: Even if developers put up buildings without taking on any debt, the poorest tenants still can't pay enough rent to cover a building's expenses. However, most affordable developments do take on debt to finance construction, putting the eventual units even further out of poor people's reach. Without a subsidy, the only housing that private developers can afford to build is for high-end customers. Income inequality only fuels the rush for developers to cater to the top of the market with luxury housing, while ignoring the middle and bottom. "There's a market failure, and the government should be stepping in to ameliorate that," Yentel says. But so far, the debate in Washington over housing is limited to helping veterans off the street or preserving the tax breaks enjoyed by wealthier homeowners.

If there is a silver lining to LA's affordable-housing crisis, it's that things have gotten so bad that the city's residents are finally paying attention. Street homelessness appears in every community; it's not just crammed into Skid Row. "We see huge amounts of activism that have sprung out of this crisis," Gross says. In the absence of assistance from the federal government, the city is attempting to patch together solutions. In November 2016, three-quarters of city voters approved Proposition HHH, an increase in property taxes to raise $1.2 billion for 10,000 units of permanent supportive housing for the homeless over the next decade. But now comes the test of whether the city can actually get the units built. "The money's there," says Paul Beesemyer, a program director at the California Housing Partnership Corporation, but "the potential gantlet of community opposition is a tough thing." Early last year, voters also approved Measure H, which raises the sales tax by a quarter of a cent and uses the money to fund homeless services.

"It's a sea change for Southern California," Beesemyer says. "We're in a fundamentally more hopeful place than we have ever been." But, he adds, "we're in a deeper hole than we've ever been in." Advocates warn that, while the money is welcome, it's a trickle in a chasm of need. "There's going to be this big influx of resources that hasn't existed in 30 years," Dennison says. "But without federal resources, none of it works."

Print Citations

CMS: Covert, Bryce. "The Deep, Uniquely American Roots of Our Affordable-Housing Crisis." In *The Reference Shelf: Affordable Housing,* edited by Micah L. Issit, 25-33. Amenia, NY: Grey House Publishing, 2019.

MLA: Covert, Bryce. "The Deep, Uniquely American Roots of Our Affordable-Housing Crisis." *The Reference Shelf: Affordable Housing,* edited by Micah L. Issit, Grey House Publishing, 2019, pp. 25-33.

APA: Covert, B. (2019). The deep, uniquely American roots of our affordable-housing crisis. In Micah L. Issit (Ed.), *The reference shelf: Affordable housing* (pp. 25-33). Amenia, NY: Grey House Publishing.

2
Affordable Housing Today

By Roy Googin, via Wikimedia.

Affordable housing units fall in and out of availability for a variety of reasons—older units fall into disrepair and are not replaced, or a developer agrees to keep a unit at an affordable rate for only a certain time span, for instance. Applicants must also fall within certain income guidelines but also be able to afford the rent on a unit, complicating whether or not they will qualify. Even if they do, the waiting lists for available housing can often be years long, and some lists are simply closed because of the housing shortage. Apartment buildings, East 57th Street, New York City.

A Growing Housing Shortage

As the affordable housing debate intensifies, politicians, pundits, and activists have identified a number of factors that contribute to the problem. Politicians and advocates may focus on one or more contributing factors when suggesting solutions, and this leads to disagreement about how to best address the problem. While some cite regional regulations and zoning as the predominant issue, others cite a lack of regulation in the real estate market, and still others have focused their attention on federal funding. Many advocates suggest that effective solutions will need to utilize a combination of measures that combine federal funding with zoning reform and local initiatives.

Regional versus National

One of the dominant themes that has emerged in studies of housing and welfare in the United States is the regional nature of the problem. The rudiments of this problem are easy to understand. Large urban centers or counties offer better employment opportunities, especially for those working in the service industries, in part because these regions support a sizable enough population that service jobs are more readily available and more lucrative.[1] The city of Chicago, Illinois, often serves as a stand-in for describing this regional pattern in the housing debate, as living within the city of Chicago is prohibitively expensive in many neighborhoods, while living in the distant suburbs is more affordable. The phenomenon that occurs in Chicago, and many other cities, is that individuals working low-paying jobs are forced to commute from the suburbs into the city for work.

Commuting drains resources and limits productivity and so mitigates the advantages of seeking employment in economically productive markets, like urban Chicago. The cost of commuting for work, school, or to access other resources can reduce resources to the point at which a family can no longer afford housing or other basic needs. Essentially, those at the lowest income levels are also those who absorb the highest cost of accessing productive economic areas and the services offered in these urban and commercial centers.[2] Further, the disadvantages for those who are forced to live far away from their jobs or from the nation's productive commercial centers can be passed down through generations. Children in these families must also commute for education or to access jobs, social opportunities, and other resources and so are at a disadvantage to the children born to families able to afford living closer to the productive areas.

The argument that individuals who can't afford living in cities should relocate to and work in more affordable areas is based on unrealistic assumptions. Communities that offer more affordable housing options are typically economically depressed. Finding local work in these areas might therefore be difficult and available jobs will typically pay lower salaries, thereby negating any benefit from reduced commuting costs. Despite these difficulties, many individuals and families do relocate to rural and suburban enclaves to find housing, and this contributes to a phenomenon called "sprawl," wherein the population economically tied to a city or other economically influential area gradually spreads further and further into surrounding land. Suburban sprawl creates a whole new set of problems for a society, often resulting in economically depressed suburbs cut off from essential urban resources and increasing the need for educational and economic assistance. Further, suburban development is far less efficient in terms of utilizing available resources and fossil fuel consumption and thus sprawl deepens the climate change problem and strains already limited resources within a state.

The housing problem is an issue that has attracted both regional and national efforts to find a solution. On the federal side, some critics believe that federal funding is an essential part of the puzzle. Some believe that the department of Housing and Urban Development (HUD) should invest in the construction of new housing projects. Among those who favor this approach, there are some who would see housing projects built in cities, while others would prefer housing to be built in underutilized counties. Critics of this approach argue that existing housing units are, in many cases, underutilized because individual who might live there cannot afford the rent. Thus, in place of engaging in new construction projects, some advocates argue that the federal government should increase financial support to offset the cost of rent and other necessities directly to individuals, who might then be in a better position to choose from existing facilities.

HUD defines affordable housing as any dwelling that an individual can occupy for less than 30 percent of their income. Measuring whether an individual or family qualifies for affordable housing therefore typically relies on the measure of Area Median Income (AMI), which is the median income calculated for all residents in an area. A person is living affordably, under this definition, if housing costs are at or below 30 percent with regard to the AMI.[3] However, this definition is problematic, because it fails to consider things like commuting costs, education costs, and healthcare costs in relation to region and proximity with regard to services. Calculations using AMI can result in situations where a low-income family can still be unable to afford a house within the "affordable" range, even if that individual or family, on paper, earns enough income to theoretically afford such a dwelling. Thus, some have argued that, instead of subsidizing construction of homes below a theoretical affordability level, families and individuals could have subsidized rent, based on a more holistic estimate of affordability.[4]

In contrast, some favor regional efforts to address housing, which can include state-funded programs to assist low-income families, subsidies for property owners who agree to utilize their properties in affordable housing programs, and a variety of other potential strategies meant to combat local and regional deficiencies and inequities in the housing market. Because housing shortages and rental prices are highly regional in nature, many see local governments as being better positioned to address the needs of consumers directly. However, in many states, funding is lacking for social assistance programs and so it is likely that a combination of federal and state funding would be necessary to create effective programs to address the housing issue.

The Nature of Neighborhoods

Another major hurdle identified by those interested in the housing debate concerns the ways in which neighborhoods, communities, regions, cities, and states develop policies that prevent the development of effective affordable housing programs. Imagine a neighborhood in which pretty much every house is a residential home, between one and three floors, with perhaps a few corner storefronts at the ends of the blocks. In the middle of one street, a few old houses have deteriorated beyond the point of repair. A real estate developer comes in and wants to build a high-rise apartment building, or a big box store, in the center of that street on the now vacant lot. Many of the residents might be resistant to this idea, whether out of concern that the development might reduce their property values, increase traffic and congestion, or might simply clash with the familiar aesthetics of their neighborhood. In such a situation, it is likely that the construction of a high-rise apartment complex or a large retail market might be prohibited by local laws that control what kind of development is permissible within a certain area. Zoning and land-use regulations evolve as communities gradually determine how best to guide the infrastructural evolution of their communities. The establishment of zoning and other land-use regulations is connected to both governmental politics and to residential preferences.

Considering the public interest side of the equation, there are those who personally oppose certain kinds of construction in areas where they either live or own property. The popular acronym NIMBY, which stands for "Not In My Backyard," refers to individuals who oppose development in their area. For instance, homeowners in a certain area may oppose proposals to build shopping centers, parking lots, highways or roads, or affordable housing itself. In some cases, these individuals may be concerned about how such construction would impact their investment, but there are a number of possible reasons why a person might fall into the NIMBY camp on a particular issue.

In many cases, individuals are interested in preserving the character or perceptive qualities of their existing neighborhoods. Zoning and construction regulations therefore sometimes evolve to include things like height limits for buildings, or specify that only certain kinds of building materials may be used. In some cases, zoning regulations can be extremely specific, designating certain types and styles of windows, colors of paint, or other details of construction. Local regulations can restrict things like swimming pools, garages or other vehicular facilities, or rules for how owners maintain the exteriors of their properties.

Zoning and land-use regulations can, in many cases, be used as a tool to exclude certain types of individuals from certain areas. For instance, some suburban communities require that any building built in the area must occupy a certain plot size. By establishing such a regulation, the residents and local government ensure that developers will not operate in their area unless they can afford the price of a certain lot size. This discourages developers from purchasing more affordable, smaller lots, and constructing more affordable houses or rental units on the property. There are also specific zoning ordinances that restrict density, essentially governing how many people can permissibly live in a certain area, and many other specific ordinances that make it prohibitive for low-income families to live in certain areas.[5]

Among the current generation of affordable housing advocates, opposition to regulations and zoning has become popular and there are many who believe that eliminating many zoning ordinances and other limits on land use could solve the affordable housing gap altogether. In some cases, combating ordinances and regulations that limit affordable housing might mean challenging local or state government policies, but it often involves sacrifices from home and property owners as well. In cases where regulatory changes might reduce property values, rental rates, or other economic benefits, residents may favor keeping regulations in place. Advocates argue that, over the longer term, creating economically diverse neighborhoods and opportunities for low-income families to build equity or gain stability has positive benefits within a community that outweigh the sacrifices in immediate profit or equity needed to enact such changes.

On the other side of the spectrum, there are communities in which residents actively invite certain kinds of development. Sometimes called YIMBY, or "Yes, In My Backyard," this camp invites and encourages certain kinds of development within their community in pursuit of certain goals. In some cases, individuals in the YIMBY camp encourage development for economic reasons and this can lead to problems for low-income residents. If development in a neighborhood advances prices too quickly, low-income renters and homeowners can find themselves effectively priced out of their own neighborhood and unable to afford rising taxes and the cost of local provisions. When this process results in the removal of minorities and/or low-income families it can be called "gentrification," a process that is ongoing in many cities around the country as developers purchase property in marginalized neighborhoods and develop properties well in advance of the local average affordability, thus shifting a neighborhood suddenly toward a different demographic and income bracket.

However, the YIMBY camp can also be a force for affordable development when neighborhoods or individuals embrace the idea of constructing affordable housing in their area. Whether or not individuals embracing the YIMBY attitudes foster positive changes is also related to the character of the affordable housing movement within each area. For instance, in some areas politicians have embraced an idea called "inclusionary zoning," which essentially enables developers to develop properties for any income market so long as the developer simultaneously agrees to set aside some property at affordable prices. Inclusionary zoning was developed in the 1970s as an antidote to exclusionary zoning practices and to generate rental properties below market rate in some of the country's productive economic regions. However, inclusionary zoning typically results in a relatively small number of affordable units being added to the market, places the onus for affordable housing directly on private developers, and typically benefits low-income families the least.[6] In some cases, inclusionary zoning might cater to the desire for social justice within certain YIMBY households, and might increase diversity within neighborhoods, but might also result in little positive benefit.

Micah L. Issitt

Works Used

"Affordable Housing." *HUD*. Housing and Urban Development. 2018. Retrieved from https://www.hud.gov/program_offices/comm_planning/affordablehousing/.

"Defining Housing Affordability." *Huduser.com*. 2018. Retrieved from https://www.huduser.gov/portal/pdredge/pdr-edge-featd-article-081417.html.

Kneebone, Elizabeth, Snyderman, Robin and Cecile Murray. "Advancing Regional Solutions to Address America's Housing Affordability Crisis." *Brookings*. The Avenue. Oct 23, 2017. Retrieved from https://www.brookings.edu/blog/the-avenue/2017/10/19/advancing-regional-solutions-to-address-americas-housing-affordability-crisis/.

Meck, Stuart, Retzlaff, Rebecca, and James Schwab. "Regional Approaches to Affordable Housing." *American Planning Association*. 2002. https://www.huduser.gov/Publications/PDF/regional_app_aff_hsg.pdf.

Reeves, Richard V. and Dimitrios Halikias. "How Land Use Regulations Are Zoning Out Low Income Families." *Brookings Institute*. Social Mobility Memos. Aug 16, 2016. Retrieved from https://www.brookings.edu/blog/social-mobility-memos/2016/08/16/zoning-as-opportunity-hoarding/.

Schneider, Benjamin. "CityLab University: Inclusionary Zoning." *CityLab*. Jul 17, 2018. Retrieved from https://www.citylab.com/equity/2018/07/citylab-university-inclusionary-zoning/565181/.

Notes

1. Mech, Retzlaff, and Schwab, "Regional Approaches to Affordable Housing."
2. Kneebone, Snyderman, and Murray, "Advancing Regional Solutions to Address America's Housing Affordability Crisis."
3. "Affordable Housing," *HUD*.
4. "Defining Housing Affordability," *Huduser.com*.
5. Reeves and Halikias, "How Land Use Regulations Are Zoning Out Low-Income Families."
6. Schneider, "CityLab University: Inclusionary Zoning."

As Affordable Housing Crisis Grows, HUD Sits on the Sidelines

By Glenn Thrush
The New York Times, July 27, 2018

WASHINGTON—The country is in the grips of an escalating housing affordability crisis. Millions of low-income Americans are paying 70 percent or more of their incomes for shelter, while rents continue to rise and construction of affordable rental apartments lags far behind the need.

The Trump administration's main policy response, unveiled this spring by Ben Carson, the secretary of housing and urban development: a plan to triple rents for about 712,000 of the poorest tenants receiving federal housing aid and to loosen the cap on rents on 4.5 million households enrolled in federal voucher and public housing programs nationwide, with the goal of moving longtime tenants out of the system to make way for new ones.

As city and state officials and members of both parties clamor for the federal government to help, Mr. Carson has privately told aides that he views the shortage of affordable housing as regrettable, but as essentially a local problem.

A former presidential candidate who said last year that he did not want to give recipients of federal aid "a comfortable setting that would make somebody want to say, 'I'll just stay here; they will take care of me,'" he has made it a priority to reduce, rather than expand, assistance to the poor, to break what he sees as a cycle of dependency.

And when congressional Democrats and Republicans scrambled to save his department's budget and rescue an endangered tax credit that accounts for nine out of 10 affordable housing developments built in the country, Mr. Carson sat on the sidelines, according to legislators and congressional staff members.

Local officials seem resigned to the fact that they will receive little or no help from the Trump administration.

"To be brutally honest, I think that we aren't really getting any help right now out of Washington, and the situation has gotten really bad over the last two years," said Chad Williams, executive director of the Southern Nevada Regional Housing Authority, which oversees public housing developments and voucher programs that serve 16,000 people in the Las Vegas area.

Nevada, ground zero in the housing crisis a decade ago, is now the epicenter of the affordability crunch, with low-income residents squeezed out of once-affordable apartments by working-class refugees fleeing from California's own rental crisis.

"I think Carson's ideas, that public housing shouldn't be multigenerational, are noble," Mr. Williams said. "But right now these programs are a stable, Band-Aid fix, and we really need them."

Underlying the conflict between Mr. Carson and officials like Mr. Williams are fundamental disagreements over the role the federal government should play.

Mr. Carson believes federal aid should be regarded only as a temporary crutch for families moving from dependency to work and sees the rent increases as a way to expand his agency's budget. Low-income renters and many local officials who run housing programs see the federal assistance as a semi-permanent hedge against evictions and homelessness that needs to be expanded in times of crisis.

This year, the White House proposed to slash $8.8 billion from the Department of Housing and Urban Development's most important housing programs. While aides say Mr. Carson privately pushed for a restoration in programs for seniors and disabled people, he publicly supported the gutting of his own department, reiterating to lawmakers last month that he felt as much responsibility toward taxpayers as tenants.

"I continue to advocate for fiscal responsibility as well as compassion," Mr. Carson told a House committee in June. He declined to comment for this article.

Under Mr. Carson's most significant policy proposal as secretary, so-called minimum rents paid by the poorest households in public housing would rise to $150 a month from $50.

His proposal has received little support from local housing operators. Over the past month, Mr. Carson has huddled with Representative Dennis A. Ross, Republican of Florida, who is drafting less stringent legislation that would allow, but not mandate, local housing authorities to raise rents and

Millions of low-income Americans are paying 70 percent or more of their income for shelter, while rents continue to rise and construction of affordable rental apartments lags far behind.

carry out reforms to streamline the process of verifying the poverty of applicants, aides said.

Still, both proposals represent a paradigm shift in federal housing policy, ending the requirement that low-income tenants spend no more than 30 percent of their net income on rent.

Tying rents to incomes has been a central part of the system since 1981, especially for the Section 8 housing voucher program, enabling 2.1 million low-income families to rent private apartments they could not otherwise afford. Mr. Carson's proposal would peg rents to 35 percent of gross income for all tenants. The Ross bill excludes voucher recipients, at the request of local housing authority officials.

"We need sensible reforms to make the system more efficient for agencies and residents," said Adrianne Todman, chief executive of the National Association of Housing and Redevelopment Officials. "But now is not the time for arbitrary federal rent hikes."

"This isn't about dependence," said Diane Yentel, president of the nonprofit National Low Income Housing Coalition, a Washington-based advocacy group that has released several recent reports documenting the affordability crunch. "Today's housing crisis is squarely rooted in the widening gap between incomes and housing costs."

And the crisis didn't begin under Mr. Trump's presidency.

Median national rents rose by 32 percent in constant dollars from 2001 to 2015, while wages remained flat, according to the Pew Charitable Trusts. The pace has picked up over the last few years, buoyed by an improving economy.

The rent increases are hitting poor and elderly people, African-Americans and low-income wage earners the hardest. A survey by the National Low Income Housing Coalition found that a worker earning the state minimum wage could afford a market-rate one-bedroom apartment in only 22 of the country's 3,000 counties.

The Obama administration initially proposed steep increases for Section 8 and other programs, but pulled back after the Republicans won control of the House in 2010.

During the 2008 campaign, Mr. Obama promised to fund an affordable housing trust fund for the construction of new units. But the $200-million-a-year program, funded by the profits of Fannie Mae and Freddie Mac, was blocked by Republican lawmakers until 2014. In 2017, it was on track to finance the construction of about 1,000 units of affordable housing in 32 states, according to federal data.

Its sister program, the Capital Magnet Fund, which has leveraged private investment to create 17,000 new units, is in the cross hairs of Mr. Trump's budget director, Mick Mulvaney, who tried to cut it by $141.7 million this year as part of his unsuccessful budget recession effort this summer.

Under Mr. Trump, funding for public housing, vouchers and new construction has risen slightly—against the president's wishes.

In March, Republican and Democratic negotiators rejected Mr. Trump's budget, adding $1.25 billion to HUD's rental assistance programs and injecting an additional $425 million to the HOME program, which funds state, local, nonprofit and private partnerships to build affordable housing.

Those moves, while significant, are likely to have a limited impact on the larger problem of the increasing number of families who cannot afford a place to live.

While prices are cooling at the high end of the market in many big cities, the low- and middle-income housing markets in Nevada, Texas, California, Florida and Colorado are so hot, local officials say, that landlords routinely reject subsidized tenants because they can charge more to other renters.

Rental construction has focused on attracting high-income tenants. From 2001 to 2013, the number of rental apartments for high-wage earners increased by 36 percent, while units for poor people shrank by nearly 10 percent, according to federal housing statistics.

With affordable stock scarce, prices are spiking. An estimated 12 million Americans, most of them poor, now spend more than half of their earnings on housing, according to HUD statistics.

One of them is Judith Toro Fortyz, 75, who receives $848 a month in Social Security and pays $594.88 of it to remain in the small two-bedroom apartment on Staten Island that she once shared with her mother.

Mrs. Toro Fortyz has been turned down for federal vouchers, reflecting a shortage in assistance that has shut out three of every four eligible applicants for Section 8. Even with an additional housing stipend from the city, she is spending 70 percent of her income on rent.

That has forced her to make wrenching decisions, like forgoing her favorite fruit, oranges, after a price spike at her local supermarket.

"I stay home a lot. I'd rather not go out because going out means you have to spend money," said Mrs. Toro Fortyz, a retired data storage worker. "I have a friend who gets Section 8 and, oh my God, they pay $200 a month. I can't even imagine having that much money to live on."

Mr. Carson's proposal alarmed many low-income tenants, especially older ones, who could face significant rent increases under the plan. "We basically wouldn't be able to get by," said Patrick Greene, 69, a retired truck driver who lives in a small HUD-subsidized apartment with his wife in Montgomery, Ala.

A more immediate threat to affordable housing, critics say, is the huge tax bill passed by Congress last year, which imperils one of the most important sources of long-term funding, the Low Income Housing Tax Credit.

Novogradac & Company, a firm that provides analytics for the construction and finance industries, estimated that demand for the $9-billion-a-year credit could dry up as investors realize savings through the tax cuts. The firm estimates that nearly 235,000 fewer apartments could be built over the next decade as a result of the tax code rewrite.

A bipartisan coalition, led by Senator Maria Cantwell, Democrat of Washington, and Senator Orrin Hatch, Republican of Utah, was able to expand the credit by an additional $400 million. But that is not likely to offset the damage done by the tax measure.

The administration is observing these efforts from the sidelines. Mr. Trump, scion of a New York real estate family that made its fortune in the 1950s and 1960s building affordable housing for white working-class neighborhoods, has shown little interest in tackling the problem.

He made only passing mention of the issue during the 2016 campaign and has pressed Mr. Carson to move more aggressively to impose work requirements on federal aid recipients.

For his part, Mr. Carson publicly acknowledges the crisis in most of his speeches. "Alarmingly high numbers of Americans continue to pay more than half of their incomes toward rent," he told a House panel in October. "Many millions remain mired in poverty, rather than being guided on a path out of it."

But he is focused less on federal solutions than on prodding local governments to ease barriers to construction. He has ordered his policy staff to come up with proposals to push local governments to reduce zoning restrictions on new projects, especially low-cost manufactured housing. HUD will also begin working with landlords around the country to come up with ways to make housing vouchers more attractive and more inclusive, aides said.

"Subsidies are a piece of the puzzle," said Raffi Williams, a spokesman for Mr. Carson, "but we must also address the regulatory barriers relative to zoning and land use in higher-cost markets that are preventing the construction of new affordable housing. This is not just a federal problem—it's everybody's problem."

Print Citations

CMS: Thrush, Glenn. "As Affordable Housing Crisis Grows, HUD Sits on the Sidelines." In *The Reference Shelf: Affordable Housing,* edited by Micah L. Issit, 43-47. Amenia, NY: Grey House Publishing, 2019.

MLA: Thrush, Glenn. "As Affordable Housing Crisis Grows, HUD Sits on the Sidelines." *The Reference Shelf: Affordable Housing,* edited by Micah L. Issit, Grey House Publishing, 2019, pp. 43-47.

APA: Thrush, G. (2019). As affordable housing crisis grows, HUD sits on the sidelines. In Micah L. Issit (Ed.), *The reference shelf: Affordable housing* (pp. 43-47). Amenia, NY: Grey House Publishing.

Closed Wait Lists and Long Waits Await Those Seeking Affordable Housing

National Low Income Housing Coalition, October 11, 2016

WASHINGTON, D.C.—Today the National Low Income Housing Coalition (NLIHC) released Housing Spotlight: A Long Wait for a Home—a report that analyzes the current state of Housing Choice Vouchers and public housing waiting lists across the country. The report paints a bleak picture of an all-too-familiar situation facing families struggling with housing affordability—closed waiting lists and long waits for assistance.

Housing Choice Vouchers (HCV) help more than 2.2 million of the lowest income families live in stable, affordable homes by covering the difference between what they can afford to pay and the cost of modest rental homes in the private market. Very few eligible families receive this needed assistance due to limited funding. In Housing Spotlight: A Long Wait for a Home, NLIHC finds that 53% of HCV waiting lists were closed to new applicants and another 4% were open only to specific populations, such as homeless individuals and families, veterans, persons with a disability, or local residents. Sixty-five percent of closed HCV waiting lists had been closed for at least one year, more than half of public housing authorities (PHAs), which administer the HCV program and public housing, did not think their lists would reopen within the next year, and wait times for HCVs often spanned years.

NLIHC's analysis shows that HCV waiting lists had a median wait time of 1.5 years for housing assistance. Twenty-five percent had a wait of at least 3 years. Twenty-five percent of the largest PHAs (5,000+ vouchers and public housing units combined) with HCV waiting lists had a wait time of at least 7 years. The average HCV waiting list consisted of 2,013 households.

Public Housing provides homes for approximately 1.1 million households. Wait lists for public housing had a median wait time of 9 months. Twenty-five percent of them had a wait time of at least 1.5 years. Public Housing waiting lists had an average size of 834 households.

HCVs and Public Housing serve our nation's lowest income renters. Extremely low income (ELI) households, whose incomes are at or below 30% of the area median income, accounted for 74% of households on the average HCV waiting list and 67% of households on the average public housing waiting list.

"Most of the poor families that are unable to obtain affordable homes spend more than half of their limited incomes on housing. They face impossible choices between paying the rent or paying for food, medicine, transportation, or child care." said NLIHC President and CEO Diane Yentel. "Congress can make more housing affordable to the lowest income people by

> **NLIHC's analysis shows that Housing Choice Vouchers (HCV) waiting lists had a median wait time of 1.5 years for housing assistance.**

significantly increasing investments in deeply targeted and highly effective tools like Housing Choice Vouchers, Public Housing and the national Housing Trust Fund."

Currently, there are several bills in Congress that would expand funding for critical affordable housing programs. These bills include the "Pathways out of Poverty Act" (H.R. 2721) and the "Common Sense Housing Investment Act" (H.R. 1662), which propose modest changes to the mortgage interest deduction to provide additional funds for both vouchers and public housing, as well as the national Housing Trust Fund; the "Ending Homelessness Act of 2016" (H.R. 4888) which would increase funding for vouchers; and the "Affordable Housing Credit Improvement Act" (S. 3237), which would better target the Low Income Housing Tax Credit program to ELI renters.

"Home is the foundation for success in every aspect of our lives. Investing in homes is an investment in education, healthcare and economic mobility," said Ms. Yentel. "As a nation, we understand the housing affordability crisis we face, we have the solutions, and we know how these solutions benefit families, communities and the economy. We lack only the political will to rebalance housing policy and target resources towards those with the greatest need. When we achieve that, we will end the long wait for a home for the nation's lowest income families."

Print Citations

CMS: "Closed Wait Lists and Long Waits Await Those Seeking Affordable Housing." In *The Reference Shelf: Affordable Housing*, edited by Micah L. Issit, 48-49. Amenia, NY: Grey House Publishing, 2019.

MLA: "Closed Wait Lists and Long Waits Await Those Seeking Affordable Housing." *The Reference Shelf: Affordable Housing*, edited by Micah L. Issit, Grey House Publishing, 2019, pp. 48-49.

APA: National Low Income Housing Coalition. (2019). Closed wait lists and long waits await those seeking affordable housing. In Micah L. Issit (Ed.), *The reference shelf: Affordable housing* (pp. 48-49). Amenia, NY: Grey House Publishing.

U.S. Housing Market Continues Rebound, Despite Increased Inequality, Says Harvard Report

By Jeff Andrews and Patrick Sisson
Curbed, June 19, 2018

The annual State of the Nation's Housing report, produced by the Joint Center for Housing Studies (JCHS) at Harvard University, offers an opportunity to step back and assess where things stand from year to year, and this year's report—the 30th Harvard has produced— paints a picture of America's housing as increasingly scarce and increasingly expensive.

Housing construction has grown every year since the housing bust in 2008, but the pace of that construction is slowing down as construction material, labor, and land have become more expensive. This has led to fewer homes being on the market, and a worsening housing shortage.

Meanwhile, with the unemployment back down to pre-crisis levels, every generation in the U.S. is looking to buy a house, creating intense demand for housing at a time when there's little supply, particularly in urban centers. The result is soaring home prices and rents that are outpacing wage growth for low- and middle-income Americans.

Here are key factors highlighted in the report, and how they're contributing to affordability problems in the U.S. housing market.

Construction Costs, Land-Use Regulation Slowing Down Housing Construction

Prior to the housing bust, the U.S. had a housing oversupply. Today, the nation faces the opposite problem—a housing shortage. While housing construction has grown every year since the housing bust, that growth is showing signs of slowing.

According to the JCHS's report, single-family housing construction starts rose by 9.4 percent in 2017, and completions rose by 8.8 percent. Multifamily housing starts, however, fell by 9.7 percent, while completions were up 11.3 percent. The report concludes that while the drop in multifamily is concerning, the pipeline for new homes remains strong.

Homebuilding has been impeded by a few factors, which have also raised the price of housing, particularly for low- and middle-income Americans. The cost of construction material has risen in aggregate by 4 percent between 2016 and 2017, led by the skyrocketing price of lumber. Labor shortages have also slowed the pace of building, in addition to raising the cost, as wages are bid up competitively. Land has gotten scarcer as well, and regulations around what builders can do with that land are preventing density increases in areas where suburban sprawl has hit a wall.

The good news is that after years of builders and developers focusing on the high-end market, construction on smaller single-family homes and manufactured housing continues to rise at a rapid pace. Still, entry-level housing is just 22 percent of single-family housing, below the average of 33 percent between 1999 and 2007.

After Years of Delaying, Millennials Enter the Homebuying Market

While housing construction is plugging along at a modest pace, housing demand has come off its post-crisis lows thanks to millennials finally entering the home-buying market. The share of millennials who live with their parents or relatives is still 26 percent, and there's another 9 percent of millennials doubled up with non-family. This means there's still likely another wave of millennials who will form new households and further increase housing demand among the generation.

Meanwhile, aging baby boomers are contributing to huge growth in the 65-and-older demographic, which has grown by more than 7 million households over the past decade. Living longer and more independently than ever, they can stay in their homes longer. As a result, there's less housing outflow from this demographic than there used to be, contributing to a shortage of existing homes for sale.

The report notes that immigrants contribute to housing demand during expansions, but more importantly, stabilize demand during downturns. Rough 1.5 million foreign-born households became homeowners between 2006 and 2016, offsetting the 1.1 million drop in native-born homeowners.

With President Trump's crackdown on legal and illegal immigration alike, the Census Bureau is projecting lower rates of immigration than prior to Trump taking office. Still, the share of population growth attributable to immigrants will grow from today's rate of 42 percent to 67 percent in 2040.

Homeownership Bounces Back Slightly, with Seniors in the Lead

Overall homeownership rates have finally turned around, buoyed by low interest rates that help first-time buyers to keep up with their mortgage. Viewed through a certain lens, 2017 was a banner year for U.S. homeownership. Roughly 1.1 million more Americans became homeowners, the highest rate since the Great Recession.

Ask anybody testing their luck this summer in the "most competitive homebuying market in history," constrained by rising home prices, affordability challenges, and a limited inventory, and they may not celebrate that milestone. Surging prices, especially in coastal metros have created stark gaps between cities.

Los Angeles's homeownership rate is 48 percent, while in Pittsburgh, it's more than 70 percent. A Los Angeles household making area median income could afford mortgages on just 11 percent of recently sold homes, while In Pittsburgh, even

> **The rental market has increasingly catered to high-end apartment dwellers while leaving lower-income renters struggling.**

a family in the lowest income group could afford 26 percent of area homes. This gap helps explains the continued lag in young adult homeownership. While the 25-34 age group saw a 0.6 percent increase in ownership last year, their 39.2 rate of homeownership is well below the 45.5 percent rate recorded 30 years earlier.

While millennials and young adults often dominate conversations about homeownership, senior citizens may actually do more to shape the market going forward. Like the U.S. population as a whole, the median age of homeowners rose, increasing from 50 in 1990 to 56 in 2016. Americans over 65 are the only age group who had a higher homeownership rate in 2017 (78.7 percent) than 1987 (75.4 percent).

The graying of homeownership has many important consequences. A 2014 survey found that 88 percent of seniors want to stay put in their current homes as they age. If they stay true to their intentions, they'll create a huge opportunity for home improvements and renovations focused on accessibility and aging in place. It also puts even more pressure on the market to provide new inventory for millennials.

Rental Housing Continues to Be a Tale of Two Worlds: Rich and Poor

The slight bump in homeownership last year was mirrored by a slight decrease in the rental population, from 36.6 to 36.1 percent of the population, with the number of renters under 35 falling by 224,000. This suggests improving financial situations have marginally improved the housing market overall, with a slight softening of the rental market.

But like last year, the rental market has increasingly catered to high-end apartment dwellers, while leaving lower-income renters struggling.

Multifamily construction continues to tilt towards the upper end, chasing an expanding market and offering more amenities (In 2016, 86 percent of new apartments had swimming pools, and 89 percent had in-unit laundry). The number of high-income renters grew last year, with those making over $100,000 increasing by 5 percent (19 percent of this demographic was renting, an all-time high). That's part of the reason multifamily construction, which delivered 336,000 new units last year, has grown at a pace not seen since the '70s.

Luxury buildings help offset the rising cost in land and construction, all big factors in sustained increases in the asking rent for new units, which ballooned from $1,090 in 2012 to $1,550 in 2017. The average asking rent for new units in Chicago, D.C., and Miami is now more than $2,000.

This stands in stark contrast to the realities faced by lower-income renters, who have seen available inventory remain essentially unchanged since 2015.

For every 100 low-income renters, only 35 rental units were affordable and available, according to the National Low-Income Housing Coalition, a shortfall of 7.2 million units. In every one of the nation's 50 major metro areas, low-income renters vastly outnumber the amount of affordable units. Conversions, demolitions, and other losses have severely cut the affordable housing inventory. More than 2.5 million units priced below $800 in real terms disappeared between 1990 and 2016.

Housing Challenges a Story of Inventory Shortfalls and Great Need among Fellow Americans

Simply put, housing is too expensive for too many Americans in too many parts of the country. Nearly a third of Americans—and 47 percent of renters—paid more than 30 percent of their income for housing in 2016. Roughly 11 million pay more than half their incomes for housing.

The strain is felt in every corner of the country, and nearly every demographic, from urban and rural to young and old (44 of renters under 30, and 54 percent of renters over 65, are cost-burdened). And the federal government is not providing nearly enough assistance.

According to HUD's Worst Case Housing Needs report, the number of renters in "very low-income households with severe cost burdens or living in inadequate or overcrowded conditions " rose from 6 to 8.3 million between 2005 and 2015, and the number of people experiencing homeless increased by 3,800 in 2017 after years of decline.

Since the first State of the Nation's Housing report 30 years ago, the number of very low-income households has increased by 6 million to 19 million nationally, all while the rental assistance and low-cost housing inventory have shrunk. Without leadership, resources, or concerted effort from all levels of government, this problem is only set to get worse.

Print Citations

CMS: Andrews, Jeff, and Patrick Sisson. "U.S. Housing Market Continues Rebound, Despite Increased Inequality, Says Harvard Law Report." In *The Reference Shelf: Affordable Housing*, edited by Micah L. Issit, 50-53. Amenia, NY: Grey House Publishing, 2019.

MLA: Andrews, Jeff, and Patrick Sisson. "U.S. Housing Market Continues Rebound, Despite Increased Inequality, Says Harvard Law Report." *The Reference Shelf: Affordable Housing,* edited by Micah L. Issit, Grey House Publishing, 2019, pp. 50-53.

APA: Andrews, J., & P. Sisson. (2019). U.S. housing market continues rebound, despite increased inequality, says Harvard law report. In Micah L. Issit (Ed.), *The reference shelf: Affordable housing* (pp. 50-53). Amenia, NY: Grey House Publishing.

10 Years After Housing Crisis: A Realtor, A Renter, Starting Over, Staying Put

By Becky Sullivan and Ari Shapiro
NPR, April 28, 2018

Ten years ago, a slow-moving disaster shook the entire country: a financial meltdown that did not leave a single state untouched.

The main catalyst was a housing bubble.

Throughout the early 2000s, housing prices in some parts of the country rose, and rose, and rose. Homes with prices that for decades had steadily grown with inflation were suddenly worth 50 percent or 100 percent more.

The rapidly rising prices fueled extraordinary behavior. Home sales nearly doubled from 2000 to 2005. In some metro areas, prices were rising so fast that an investor could buy a house, sit on it for a couple months, and sell it for a profit.

For many homeowners, rising values made it attractive to refinance their mortgages and use their home equity to pay for other things—investment properties, remodels, cars.

Lenders let people pay more than they could afford for homes and devised extraordinary methods of doing so: loans described as "NINJA" (no income, no job, no assets), "liar" (no-verification "stated income" loans) and "exploding" (loans where the monthly payments would "explode" after a two-year promotional rate). Subprime lending soared.

Then the bubble popped.

In 2007, home prices started to tumble. Homeowners began to default, leading to record foreclosures. Lenders and banks were left holding bad debt.

Major financial institutions began to fail, one by one: In January 2008, mortgage lender Countrywide was sold to Bank of America; Bear Stearns was bailed out in March and sold to JPMorgan Chase; in September, Lehman Brothers collapsed and Washington Mutual became the largest bank failure in U.S. history. In October, Congress passed a $700 billion bailout bill.

Officially, the recession lasted only until June 2009. But wages tumbled and unemployment soared well past then. By February 2010, the U.S. economy had lost 8.8 million jobs from the peak in late 2007.

Phoenix felt the housing collapse worse than almost anywhere else. On average, homes in the metro area lost 56 percent of their value—the third worst in the country.

The meltdown in prices left hundreds of thousands of homeowners underwater on their mortgages, owing more than their houses were worth. Some chose to stay in their homes. Some walked away by choice. Many were forced to leave. Foreclosures swept across the city by the tens of thousands.

Ten years later, America has rebounded from the Great Recession and the housing crash. The stock market has recovered. Unemployment is lower than it was during the housing bubble.

In Phoenix, the scars remain.

The Realtor

Every time I hear a smoke detector beeping like the battery's dead, I have a flashback of the crash. So in my house when a smoke detector starts beeping, I am up and I get on a ladder and I'm changing that thing because all I have is visions of the past.

"I've seen a lot over 27 years," Sean Hahn says. At 50, he has spent more than half his life working as a Realtor in Phoenix, since the early 1990s. There has been a lot to see in Phoenix real estate in that time. During the housing bubble, local housing prices doubled in just three years. "We'd put a house on the market, and by noon we'd have 12 offers," Hahn says.

Then came the crash.

Clients Hahn had helped buy a house a year or two before began to call about exit strategies. He learned how to negotiate short sales, helping homeowners come to an agreement with their bank to sell the house for less than they still owed. Hahn is upbeat, naturally optimistic. The change haunted him.

"I had a stomachache all the time when I was working through that process," he says. "They'd invested so much time and money in making it a home, and now they have to leave it. I still have nightmares to this day that I'm going through that."

During the bust, Hahn would go out driving with investors, looking up foreclosed homes and evaluating their condition. Sometimes the departing owners would clean the place before leaving. More often, they did not. Hahn saw properties that had been stripped of cabinetry, doors, air conditioners, copper pipes, even the lightbulbs. The worst were the houses that had been intentionally defaced by their desperate, angry former owners.

Out of them all, Hahn says there is one abandoned house he remembers most.

In 2012, he and an investor were driving around town inspecting foreclosed homes.

One house on their list, a small ranch about 20 miles north of downtown, reeked so strongly of urine that they could smell it from the driveway. The investor told Hahn, "Let's go; this looks horrible."

But Hahn wanted to take a look: It was the first house he'd ever bought for himself. He and his wife purchased the house in the late '80s for $55,000 and moved out a few years later. Now, it was next to ruined.

"It was so sad. It was just, like, destruction and damage where people just let go. They just lived in filth. They destroyed the house," he says. "My wife and I had so much pride in that little home."

The Former Homeowner

I tell people money is the root of all evil. Honestly, it was just a blame game. It just got ugly, to where you just don't know what to blame, you just don't know what to do.

In October 1999, Adriana Rodriguez and her then-husband bought a comfortable house in a decent part of Phoenix for themselves and their two young daughters. She did administrative work in a dental office; he was a forklift operator for warehouses.

In 2005, they refinanced their mortgage to make some upgrades to the house. But, she acknowledges now, "We didn't understand the loan quite completely." After a few years, their interest rate jumped, and their mortgage payments skyrocketed.

About 80 percent of all subprime mortgages written during the peak of the housing bubble were what was known as "exploding" adjustable-rate mortgages. Lenders offered two or three years at an introductory teaser rate. Then, interest rates would jump as much as 4 percentage points, and the borrower's monthly payments would skyrocket. Rodriguez says she believes they were taken advantage of.

Multiple analyses of home loans initiated during the housing boom have found that black and Latino borrowers were more likely to receive high-risk loans than whites with similar incomes and credit scores. And once they had the subprime loans, blacks and Hispanics were often charged higher interest rates than were white subprime borrowers with similar credit scores, according to a study by the Center for Responsible Lending, a nonprofit research group.

Experts disagree on how much blame for the crisis should be placed on subprime lenders. Only about 5 percent of housing mortgage applications approved in 2006 were subprime. The racial disparities in lending practices helped drive foreclosure rates higher for borrowers of color. And mortgage discrimination persists today.

As the Rodriguezes' mortgage payments ballooned, the economy collapsed. Her husband lost his job in 2008. They began to struggle to hold together their marriage. In the end, they divorced, leaving Adriana Rodriguez to pay for the house on her own. She sold her car to help with home payments, but she was only delaying the inevitable. In 2010, she defaulted on the payments, and she and her daughters moved out within a year. They've rented ever since.

Now, at 42 years old, Rodriguez says the thought of buying a new house is daunting.

"I just don't even want to go there," she says. "I have friends who have recovered from it and have purchased homes. But I don't know where to start. It's just hard. You don't ever want to go through that again."

The Boomerang Buyers

We just realized, this truly is something that is going to bury us. And I think then we got more serious about the idea of, 'Let's make the mistake. Let's own the mistake and move on. And then we'll not make that again.'

In 2006, Kristin and Justin Hege bought the house they thought would be their "forever home." At the time, she was 29 and he was 27. It felt perfect: the right size, the right location. They brought one of their sons home from the hospital to that house.

"I grew up in a small town in Ohio," Kristin says. "The 'forever home' thing was a legit thing. You stayed in your house until your kids went away to school."

Expecting to stay in the house for 15 years or more, they decided to do a complete remodel in 2007. They refinanced their original mortgage

> The racial disparities in lending practices helped drive foreclosure rates higher for borrowers of color. And mortgage discrimination persists today.

to pull out some equity to make the renovations. Afterward, at the height of the bubble, their house was valued at more than $400,000.

When home prices began to fall, their initial reaction was to stick it out. They could have kept paying their mortgage. The Heges own their own businesses; they were very sensitive to the damage a foreclosure or a short sale could do to their credit. And they thought it felt wrong to walk away from a commitment they'd signed on to.

"We could have each had two more jobs apiece and made it work and done it," Kristin says. "It was very hard for us and who we are as people to walk away."

But as home prices kept falling, the financial reality became impossible to ignore.

Eventually the Heges sold their house in a short sale for $149,000—about half of what they still owed to the bank. (In a typical short sale, the bank agrees to accept less than what is owed and release the remainder of the debt. In many cases, lenders prefer short sales over foreclosures.)

Events like short sales can stay on a credit report for seven years. Because of that, many Americans who missed payments, sold short or went into foreclosure during the recession are now returning to the housing market with healthy credit. They are called "boomerang buyers."

After seven years of renting, the Heges bought again for the first time last year.

"Anyone can make a mistake. We made a mistake. We made a dumb choice," Justin says. "We are much more fiscally responsible now. Seven years is a long time to learn."

The Locksmith

In my business, you normally aren't going into people's homes without them there. So to be able to see a window into what life was like for those families at their worst and the things that they decided to leave—it was heartbreaking at times; it was disgusting at times.

In 2007, Fred Decker was tired of his job managing a Starbucks. He was 32. He quit and became a locksmith.

Soon, Decker was spending his days changing the locks on vacant homes, as many as eight a day. Eventually, he says, he changed the locks on two-thirds of the homes in his own neighborhood.

The first step was to check whether anyone was there. He would peer in the windows, put his ear to the door. A beeping smoke detector was a dead giveaway—the batteries had gone dead, but no one was around to change them. If the house was vacant, he would pick the lock on the front door and go in.

Foreclosures came in all conditions. Some were impeccably cleaned; some were trashed. Most were in between, with leftover clothes or furniture here and there, cotton swabs on the floor or beer bottles on the table.

In one house, he remembers, right by the front door was an end table with Halloween candy in it. It was August.

"It just looked like they vanished," he says. The house was completely furnished. There were pictures on the walls, bills on the counter. "The most unsettling thing was the clothes still being in the dressers, in the closets. They were just gone."

Decker is a homeowner himself. He and his wife bought their house in 2006. At the time, they thought they were getting a deal. They bought from a friend who needed to sell in a hurry and ended up buying the house for about $30,000 less than its appraised value.

In reality, there could not have been a worse time to buy a house in Phoenix. As they bought the house, prices began stalling; soon after, they began to crater. The Deckers were underwater by 2007. At the bottom of the trough, their home was worth half of what they had bought it for.

He and his wife chose to stay. He says their mortgage was a contract they had made with society, that it would be irresponsible, even immoral, to walk away.

But every time his job took him into a foreclosed home, he was faced with his own decision to stay.

"I felt like a sucker. Like, here I am, paying my bills, and everyone else—I don't know," he says. "Are they in a situation where they lost their jobs and they just had no choice? Or are they like some people that I know who just decided, 'Well, this is a bad situation. I don't want to be underwater for 10 years; I'm just going to walk'?"

Decker and his wife are still living in the same house. They hope to be above water next year.

Print Citations

CMS: Sullivan, Becky. "10 Years After Housing Crisis: A Realtor, A Renter, Starting Over, Staying Put." In *The Reference Shelf: Affordable Housing*, edited by Micah L. Issit, 54-59. Amenia, NY: Grey House Publishing, 2019.

MLA: Sullivan, Becky. "10 Years After Housing Crisis: A Realtor, A Renter, Starting Over, Staying Put." *The Reference Shelf: Affordable Housing*, edited by Micah L. Issit, Grey House Publishing, 2019, pp. 54-59.

APA: Sullivan, B. (2019). 10 years after housing crisis: A realtor, a renter, starting over, staying put. In Micah L. Issit (Ed.), *The reference shelf: Affordable housing* (pp. 54-59). Amenia, NY: Grey House Publishing.

Will the Housing Bubble Cause Another Financial Crisis?

By Jeff Andrews
Curbed, May 2, 2018

At a recent doctor's appointment I told my physician about a story I'm working on that involves the securitization of loans in which the underlying collateral is housing, evoking the dreaded term "mortgage-backed securities."

My doctor's reaction was something I've heard several times from friends and family lately: "They're doing the same things that caused the financial crisis!"

In a lot ways that is true; much of the financial machinery that produced mortgage-backed securities and their derivatives are still in place, churning out the same products that wreaked havoc on the global economy.

But there a few key differences between the housing market then and the housing market today that make another global financial calamity, or at least one that mirrors the previous one, unlikely.

While highly complex debt instruments such as mortgage-back securities, collateralized debt obligations, and credit-default swaps are what turned the housing crash into a financial crash, the underlying problem was ultimately quite simple: Low- and moderate-income people were given mortgages on which default wasn't just possible or even probable, but inevitable.

In the early 2000s, the construction sector churned out houses at a dizzying pace, leading to an oversupply of single-family homes. To get people into these homes, lenders extended credit to people who shouldn't have gotten it, and the terms of the mortgages were such that the interest rates would "reset" after a couple years.

The process was egged on by Wall Street, which catered to intense global demand for mortgage-backed securities from investors both foreign and domestic. The explosion of these securities created demand from hedge funds and insurance companies for credit-default swaps and other derivatives, which served as insurance policies against their mortgage-backed securities.

The frenzy pushed home prices up, and everyone in the chain was getting rich on transaction fees without regard for whether the mortgage payments actually came in. When the interest rates on subprime mortgages began to "reset" to higher rates in 2007, defaults sky-rocketed, the securities failed, and the whole system came crashing down.

Today, all this financial machinery still exists, with one key difference—subprime mortgage loans with adjustable rates aren't being written at anywhere close to the same volume. This isn't necessarily the result of newfound restraint by

> **Today, all this financial machinery still exists, with one key difference—subprime mortgage loans with adjustable rates aren't being written at anywhere close to the same volume.**

mortgage lenders and Wall Street bankers; it's more a reflection of a housing market that's the inverse of the one that existed in the run-up to the collapse.

Instead of a housing oversupply that required creative lending to attract buyers, today we have a housing shortage that's creating an affordability crisis. Homes for sale in some of the hotter markets in the U.S. spark intense bidding wars usually won by the person with the most cash or the best credit. What realtor is going to sell a home to someone who needs a subprime mortgage when they can pick and choose between multiple offers that are more than likely going to include someone with good credit?

In addition, almost 90 percent of the mortgage-backed securities today are produced by the "government-sponsored" mortgage facilitators Freddie Mac, Fannie Mae, and Ginnie Mae, compared to roughly half in the run up to the housing collapse. Those enterprises now have strict credit guidelines for the mortgages they package into their mortgage-backed securities.

Most mortgage lenders don't hold the loans the write; they sell them to Fannie Mae or Freddie Mac so they can redeploy that money into a new loan. They make money off the transaction, not on the incoming mortgage payment. But they can't sell the mortgages to Fannie or Freddie if they don't conform to Fannie or Freddie's rules. For the most part, this forces banks and mortgage lenders into better lending practices.

While it looks like things are stable now, that doesn't mean it can't change in a hurry. One of the remarkable things about the financial crisis is how quickly the bubble was inflated. Bad, adjustable-rate loans started seeping into the market in 2005, and three years later the economy was in free fall.

Already we're seeing an uptick in subprime mortgage bonds produced by private lenders, although it's grown from barely a tiny blip into a slightly larger tiny blip. In 2014, $100 *million* in mortgage-backed securities was issued. In just the first half of 2017, $2.6 *billion* in subprime mortgage-backed securities were issued in the $53.5 billion mortgage-backed securities market. Even if all the new subprime mortgage bonds failed, financial markets would hardly notice. In 2006, there was almost $1.5 *trillion* in outstanding subprime mortgage debt.

In the run up to the crisis, easy credit created an artificial demand for housing that pushed prices up, creating a bubble that ultimately burst. Today, millennials looking to become first-time home buyers are flooding a housing market that's starved for supply. Low supply and high demand means high prices. One could argue that today's housing bubble isn't a bubble at all, but a reflection of an incredible supply and demand imbalance.

There are so many institutions and industries that depend on home prices going up that there are intense institutional and policy forces causing just that. If they haven't already, those forces may push prices beyond the real value of the asset. Wall Street being Wall Street, it's found new ways to squeeze every last dollar out of the housing market by leveraging big data and national online investor platforms such as those for home flipper loans and so-called iBuyers.

The financialization of housing by institutional capital has negative consequences, like inflating home values at a time when affordable housing is scarce to nonexistent. And as housing is such a bedrock of the U.S. economy, the well-being of housing and the economy are tethered such that if one goes down, the other goes down with it.

It may over the next few years turn out that these forces inflate a housing bubble—and that bubble might burst, causing an economic down turn. The inverse could happen, too. But given changes to lending practices and the mortgage securitization chain, the bubble probably won't burst in the same way it did last time around.

Print Citations

CMS: Andrews, Jeff. "Will the Housing Bubble Cause Another Financial Crisis?" In *The Reference Shelf: Affordable Housing*, edited by Micah L. Issit, 60-62. Amenia, NY: Grey House Publishing, 2019.

MLA: Andrews, Jeff. "Will the Housing Bubble Cause Another Financial Crisis?" *The Reference Shelf: Affordable Housing*, edited by Micah L. Issit, Grey House Publishing, 2019, pp. 60-62.

APA: Andrews, J. (2019). Will the housing bubble cause another financial crisis? In Micah L. Issit (Ed.), *The reference shelf: Affordable housing* (pp. 60-62). Amenia, NY: Grey House Publishing.

3
Exploring the Affordable Housing Debate

Microsoft's $500 million plan to build housing in Seattle is one of a number of recent tech company forays into the housing problem. While some view this as a welcome private-sector substitute for dwindling federal involvement, others fear the creation of modern-day "company towns" and are not comfortable relying on tech companies for such a basic societal need. The west campus of the Microsoft Redmond campus.

History of Policy Approaches

Affordable housing is an idea that has emerged repeatedly in human history and in cultures around the world. The basic premise is to invest public and/or government revenue or to regulate industry so as to extend the benefit of safe and secure housing to as many members of society as possible, at all levels of the income spectrum. The effort to create affordable housing has been ongoing in the United States since the nineteenth century and reflects the realization that America's economic system can result in wide-ranging outcomes for individuals. While a few enjoy economic mobility and increasing wealth, the vast majority experience stagnant earning potential.

The Ability to Afford Housing

The cost of housing varies according to many different factors. Supply and demand impacts housing prices and availability, but so do interest rates, economic growth, and wage growth. Investigations of the housing and rental markets in the 2010s indicate that America is in the midst of a housing crisis, resulting from a combination of issues including zoning and exclusionary policies and a lack of governmental investment. The affordable housing issue is also inextricably linked to wage and income stagnation. A 2014 study found that the wealthiest 1 percent of Americans have seen their income grow by 128.9 percent between 1979 and 2011, while average income growth for the remaining 99 percent of Americans grew by only 2.3 percent, from $41,751 to $42,694. This means that the wealthiest 1 percent have garnered more than 88 percent of all income growth over much of the last half century.[1]

Unequal income growth means that fewer and fewer Americans can afford things like housing, food, transportation, health care, and education. Over time, many American states, cities, and other communities have engaged in efforts to reduce the exploitation of the poor and working class or to utilize the collective resources of the community to expand access to the benefits of economic participation. The fact that many economists and social welfare activists today see an affordable housing crisis indicates, however, that efforts since the 1800s have been largely insufficient to address the problem.

Shaping the Public Housing Debate

The growth of America's cities, driven by the emergence of factory and manufacturing jobs, combined with the massive influx of immigrants into America's urban centers, exposed a critical housing shortage in the 1800s. While it might seem that increased demand would simply result in a building boom, most Americans were living in poverty and had little to spend on housing. Nonetheless, real estate privateers did seek to profit from the situation. In many cases, single-family homes were divided into tenement housing, with three or more families living in a building constructed for one. Other developers exploited the situation with low-quality apartment complexes lacking even basic amenities, recognizing that the growing and desperately poor public was essentially left with few options. The tenements and slums of America's cities at the turn of the century have become a familiar part of American lore. Cramped, crowded, crime-ridden, and failing to meet even the most basic standards of hygiene, they were the result of an exploitative private real estate industry unrestrained by government. Calls for regulation in the states and federal government met with resistance from conservatives who argued that free-market forces would eventually change the situation. A coalition of state advocates initiated the first efforts to utilize collective revenues to improve the conditions for the working-class poor.

The first effort to address the welfare of America's tenement residents was the New York Housing Act of 1879; its goal was to make tenements safer. Investigations had shown that many of the buildings lacked ventilation, fire safety provisions, and plumbing, and the New York State government undertook efforts to address these issues, forcing builders to sacrifice some profit in order to meet basic safety needs. The commissioner of New York City's Tenement House Department stated of tenement housing that "there can be no question that the three great scourges of mankind, disease, poverty, and crime, are in a large measure due to bad housing."[2] Other east coast cities adopted similar provisions, which protected consumers from only the most egregious forms of corporate exploitation.

The federal government was not involved with housing until World War I. The US Shipping Act of 1917, passed under the Woodrow Wilson administration, appropriated $100 million to build more than 16,000 homes. While the effort was marketed as an effort to address social welfare, the project was deeply compromised by the interest of factories and other companies. By creating housing projects surrounding factories, and often isolated from other communities, the government and industry leaders worked together to create a captive workforce. A 1918 essay in the *Journal of the American Institute of Architects* summarized the situation by stating, "Except in towns where there is great diversity of employment, the effect is to tie the worker to the mill-owner like a feudal peasant to his lord. It interferes with the mobility of labor." The welfare director of a mill that benefitted from one of the government's housing projects stated that the project would "let them [workers] invest their savings in their homes and own them. Then they won't leave and they won't strike. It ties them down so that they have a stake in our [the company's] prosperity."[3]

The next major federal effort to address the housing issue came through Franklin Roosevelt's efforts to address the surge in poverty and homelessness that accompanied the Great Depression of the 1930s. The Public Works Administration (PWA) was created in 1933 as part of the National Industrial Recovery Act and participated in the construction of more than 25,000 units in 58 separate areas over a 40-year period. One of the pioneers in housing development in the 1930s was

Catherine Bauer, author of the 1934 book *Modern Housing*. Bauer believed that government housing projects needed to be large-scale and built entirely by nonprofit or collaborative entities without the input or involvement of private-sector builders. She further explained that they needed to be aimed at creating communities for individuals at all levels of the income spectrum where the consistent quality of the homes would, in ways, disguise the differences in income levels. Bauer believed that by removing the stigma of affordable or low-income housing, individuals at all levels of the income spectrum could access the positive benefits of home ownership and community integration.

Bauer participated with legislators to create a public housing program in 1935 and 1936, resulting in the passage of the US Housing Act in 1937. However, in the political debate that followed, the legislation was compromised, and the altered approach that emerged has defined federal housing initiatives into the modern era. Lobbyists for the commercial realty industry successfully developed key provisions that ensured that public housing would be eligible only to low-income families, thus creating low-income communities rather than economically diverse communities. Further, lobbyists succeeded in limiting the costs of public housing developments and ensured that public housing would only be constructed where blighted real estate was cleared. Essentially, this meant that public housing would be separate from the broader community, inferior in quality and construction, and only constructed in areas that had limited economic viability, as evinced by the blighted properties cleared to make way for the new construction project.[4]

Mid-Century to New Century

In the United States, interest in addressing housing issues peaks during periods of social or economic turbulence. The most significant efforts to address housing issues occurred in the periods surrounding World War I, World War II, and the Great Depression. The social tumult of the 1960s brought about a different kind of affordable housing movement tied to the broader issue of institutionalized racism. The Department of Housing and Urban Development (HUD) was created during this time and was intended to create a permanent federal voice and influence in the nation's housing issues, while the Civil Rights Act of 1968, which also included the Fair Housing Law (Title VIII), was the first time that the federal government intervened in an effort to prohibit racial and class discrimination in the real estate industry. That same year, the Housing Act created the Government National Mortgage Association (Ginnie Mae), which was intended to expand mortgage availability to middle-income families in an effort to increase home ownership and (perceptively) community or social investment.

Between 2007 and 2010, the United States suffered a major recession, in part related to what economists and the media have called the "subprime mortgage crisis." The effort to increase home ownership was one factor that led to the crisis, as lenders expanded their consumer market by packaging mortgages into pools and selling interest to investors, a system called private-label mortgage-backed securities (PMBS). This increased the pool of first-time homebuyers and encouraged banks and other lenders to risk giving mortgages to high-risk clients. With demand for property growing, housing prices increased, and investors in PMBS at first profited from this system until housing prices peaked and subprime mortgage lenders started to hit financial difficulties. As fewer individuals were able to sell or refinance to reduce debt, foreclosures increased, thereby flooding the market with even more property even as demand was falling. Ultimately, the 2007-2010 crisis was a major contributor to the recession that decreased consumer wealth, increased homelessness and poverty, and weakened trust in the consumer banking and real-estate markets.[5]

While it is widely acknowledged that there is a housing crisis, at least in some parts of the United States, there is far less agreement about how to address the issue. In the past, consumers have been marginalized by real estate industry lobbying and, arguably, the greed of individuals seeking to profit from real estate trends at the expense of public welfare. The needs of America's poor and of families suffering from various types of housing insecurity have therefore been sacrificed by politicians who chose to prioritize corporate interests, or who have embraced the concept that free-market competition will influence the evolution of the industry to benefit consumers.[6]

Writing in the *Journal of Housing and Community Development,* Betsey Martens argues that housing policy initiatives in American history have rarely emerged from "an authentic vision of doing anything remarkable for families sidelined by the market." Rather, Martens argues that policy changes have been motivated by either a desire to build the economy, and thus to aid private-sector developers and businesses, or to shape or control public behavior, as in the early efforts to address the problems with tenements out of the belief that doing so would address crime and other sociological issues. Martens argues that "public housing has been disabled by genuine and disingenuous attempts to fix it since its compromised 1937 birth, we need a new paradigm if there is to be place-based housing for very low-income Americans in the twenty-first century."[7]

Micah L. Issitt

Works Used

Biles, Roger. *From Tenements to Taylor Homes: In Search of an Urban Housing Policy in Twentieth-Century America.* University Park: The Pennsylvania University Press, 2000.

Childs, Richard S. "What Is a House?" in Whitaker, Ackerman, Child, and Wood, eds, *The Housing Problem in War and in Peace.* Washington, DC: Journal of the American Institute of Architects, 1918.

Edson, Charles L. "Affordable Housing—An Intimate History." *Journal of Affordable Housing and Community Development Law.* Winter 2011. Retrieved from http://apps.americanbar.org/abastore/products/books/abstracts/5530024%20chapter%201_abs.pdf.

Martens, Betsey. "A Political History of Affordable Housing." *Journal of Housing & Community Development.* January/February 2009. Retrieved from http://

content.csbs.utah.edu/~fan/fcs5400-6400/studentpresentation2009/03Reading_3.pdf.

Sommeiller, Estell and Mark Price. *The Increasingly Unequal States of America: Income Inequality by State, 1917 to 2011.* Economic Analysis and Research Network (EARN). Feb 19, 2014.

Zestos, George K. *The Global Financial Crisis: From US Subprime Mortgages to European Sovereign Debt.* New York: Routledge, 2016.

Notes

1. Sommeiller and Price, *The Increasingly Unequal States of America.*
2. Biles, *From Tenements to Taylor Homes*, 25.
3. Childs, "What Is a House?" 55.
4. Martens, "A Political History of Affordable Housing."
5. Zestos, *The Global Financial Crisis.*
6. Edson, "Affordable Housing—An Intimate History."
7. Martens, "A Political History of Affordable Housing."

Housing in the US Is Too Expensive, Too Cheap, and Just Right: It Depends on Where you Live

By Cecile Murray and Jenny Schuetz
The Brookings Institution, June 21, 2018

Housing costs are an immediate concern to many U.S. families and to policymakers. If people spend "too much" on housing (defined by HUD as more than 30 percent of their income), they may not be able to afford other necessities, such as food or health care. Cities and towns with high housing costs are particularly tough for young families, who tend to have lower incomes and wealth. Conversely, communities with unusually low housing prices can also be problematic, especially for long-term homeowners, who rely on housing wealth to pay for their children's education or to supplement retirement savings.

Assessing whether housing costs are too high or too low is somewhat subjective. One shorthand measure is the ratio of house prices to household income: historically, U.S. median house prices have been roughly 2.5 to 4 times median income. (What price is "affordable" to a buyer with a given income depends partly on mortgage terms, such as the loan-to-value ratio, interest rate, and share of income spent on housing.)[1]

In this analysis, we investigate the distribution of neighborhood house price-to-income ratios across the U.S., focusing especially on locations with unusually high or low ratios.[2] Both incomes and housing market fundamentals—such as land availability, development costs, wages, and demographics—vary by geography. This analysis helps identify regions of the country where house prices are "too high" and "too low," where middle-income households have to stretch to buy homes, and where homeowners find it difficult to build housing wealth. Because housing prices vary substantially within as well as across metropolitan areas, the analysis focuses on price-income ratios at the neighborhood (census tract) level. This allows us to look for within-metro patterns; for instance, comparing neighborhoods in the urban core to those in suburban areas.

One important caveat: our analysis considers housing affordability primarily for families in the middle of the income distribution. Prior research shows that the poorest 20 percent of U.S. households have difficulty paying their rent without foregoing other necessities, regardless of where they live.

House Prices Are Affordable to Middle-Income Households in Most U.S. Neighborhoods

In the median U.S. neighborhood, house prices are approximately three times annual household income. This matches expectations about how much individual families can spend to buy a home without putting themselves in financial jeopardy. A majority of Americans live in neighborhoods where home price-income ratios are between 2.5 and 4.[3] Neighborhoods with headline-grabbing high price-income ratios are rare: about five percent of the nation's neighborhoods have ratios above eight. Another five percent of neighborhoods have price-income ratios below 1.7.

Affordability Is Mostly a Problem in Large Northeastern and Western Cities

Because housing markets are fundamentally local, the national statistics mask substantial variation across different parts of the U.S. Almost all Southern and Midwestern households live in affordable neighborhoods, while large shares of Northeastern and Western neighborhoods have price-income ratios that would stretch middle-income family budgets. The South and West have larger shares of neighborhoods with unusually low price-income ratios, places where owning a home is unlikely to result in building wealth.

Housing affordability also varies across cities, suburbs, small towns, and rural areas.[4] Highly unaffordable neighborhoods are most concentrated in the urban core of large metropolitan areas. Urban centers tend to have a highly diverse housing stock, with buildings of different ages, sizes, and architectural styles. Cities also have a wide range of incomes, with very poor and very wealthy families often living in close proximity. Both of these trends combine to give urban neighborhoods a wide dispersion of housing price-income ratios, with greater concentration of neighborhoods at both the high and low end of the distribution. Suburbs of large metropolitan areas—where the majority of U.S. families live—have lower average price-income ratios, as well as fewer neighborhoods with outlying ratios. The distribution of price-income ratios is narrowest for neighborhoods outside metropolitan areas (small towns and rural areas). Non-metropolitan areas also have the largest share of neighborhoods with unusually low price-income ratios.

Premium for Oceans, Discount for Great Lakes

Urban economists and real estate agents have long known that people will pay a premium for locations with special amenities, such as nice weather or scenic views. Proximity to large bodies of water offers both outdoor recreation and pretty scenery. Consistent with predictions, metro areas near saltwater coasts—the Atlantic and Pacific Oceans and the Gulf of Mexico—have higher price-income ratios.[5] However, metro areas around the Great Lakes ("freshwater") have somewhat lower neighborhood price-income ratios than either saltwater coasts or inland regions. (Note that the analysis compares all neighborhoods within water-adjacent metro areas to all neighborhoods in inland regions, rather than comparing neighborhoods at different distance to water within the same metro area.) Saltwater coastal metros have higher price-income ratios relative to inland or freshwater areas within census regions as well.

Which Communities Have the Largest Share of "Too Cheap" Neighborhoods? Which Communities Are "Too Expensive"?

Neighborhoods with persistently low home price-income ratios raise concerns about the ability of families to build wealth because home equity is the main source of wealth for middle-income families. Notably, disparate rates of return on home-ownership contribute to the racial wealth gap.

Metropolitan areas with low price-income ratios are located in very different parts of the country from high-priced metropolitan areas. The lowest ratio metros are mostly located in the Midwest, especially clustered around the Great Lakes, and scattered across Texas. The metros with the highest ratios are primarily along the Pacific and Northeast Atlantic coasts. South Florida, Colorado, and several smaller metros along the Southeast coast also rank among the most expensive areas. Across the U.S., most states have more metro areas with price-income ratios in the normal range (2.4-4.3) than metros with outlying values.

An alternative way to think about "cheap" versus "expensive" metros is to calculate the share of neighborhoods within each metro that have unusually high or low price-income ratios. This metric is useful because two metros could have similar average price-income ratios but different shares of low- and high-value

> **Local governments broke their own housing markets, and they will have to fix them.**

neighborhoods. As has been widely covered by the media, Californian and Hawaiian communities stand out for having the largest shares of "too expensive" neighborhoods. By contrast, the five metro areas with the largest shares of "too cheap" neighborhoods are located in Illinois, Michigan, and Pennsylvania—a geographic pattern that has received less media attention. Large cities such as Flint, Mich. and Los Angeles have many neighborhoods with extreme price-income ratios, but some mid-sized and smaller communities, such as Danville, Ill. and Santa Cruz, Calif., share that characteristic.

Policy Implications

The spatial patterns of house price-income ratios suggest three avenues of improvement for policy—and highlights the need for coordination across different levels of government.

Public policies should not favor homeownership over other means of wealth building. Heartland cities and small towns have seen largely flat or falling real housing prices: this makes them affordable places to buy a home, but also means they are challenging places to build wealth through homeownership. As we saw during the Great Recession, low housing prices can trap families in place if they owe more on their mortgages than potential sale price of home. In low-priced areas, even families that have paid down their mortgages find it difficult to build wealth. That makes it harder for them to supplement retirement savings or borrow against home equity for their kids' education. Federal tax policies that strongly favor owner-occupied homes over other asset types are not well suited to support middle-class wealth building in lower-price locations.

Housing unaffordability for middle-income households is a regional rather than a national problem. Nearly all communities have some neighborhoods that will be out of reach for middle-income families—the "nicest" neighborhood in town. But in most communities, middle-income households can still afford to buy a home in a reasonably wide range of neighborhoods. Because the problem is mostly regional, responsibility for policy solutions rests primarily with state and local governments.

Local governments broke their own housing markets, and they will have to fix them. Evidence suggests that in many of the Northeastern and Western communities where price-income ratios are highest, those high housing prices result from excessive land use regulation—that is, from policy choices of local governments. Making housing more affordable to middle-income families requires those same governments to revise their zoning and allow more housing to be built, especially near jobs and transportation. States can encourage better local regulation through carrots and sticks, if they figure out the politics. At the federal level, HUD could more effectively use its bully pulpit to call out communities that obstruct new housing, and share information on how to build housing more cheaply.

Future articles will explore in more detail how federal, state, and local agencies can each contribute to better-functioning housing markets.

Footnotes

1. Standard assumptions used in the literature are that a buyer will spend 30% of income on principal, interest, taxes and insurance and make a 20% downpayment. Interest rates have been at historic lows for the past decade, allowing buyers to purchase homes at higher multiples of their income. Varying these three parameters—income spent on housing, LTV, and interest rate—gives a range of possible price-income ratios for between 2.6 and 5.3.

2. House prices are estimated using value of owner-occupied homes from the ACS. Although self-reported housing values often differ from observed sales prices, tract-level data from actual transactions are not available.

3. We use Census tracts as a proxy for neighborhoods, and we exclude tracts where fewer than 10 percent of housing units are owner-occupied.

4. We define urban Census tracts as those that fall inside the first-named city in the official title of one of the nation's most populous 100 metropolitan areas, or any other city in the title that has a population of at least 100,000. We classify all other Census tracts in the largest 100 metro areas as suburban, and

Census tracts in other metropolitan areas as small metro. Lastly, we classify Census tracts that do not fall inside any metro area as rural.

5. Metropolitan areas are defined as "saltwater" if the centroid is within 75 miles of the Atlantic or Pacific Oceans or the Gulf of Mexico. Metropolitan areas within 75 miles of a Great Lake are defined as "freshwater." All remaining metropolitan areas are defined as "inland." Tracts outside metropolitan areas are not categorized.

Print Citations

CMS: Murray, Cecile, and Jenny Schuetz. "Housing in the US Is Too Expensive, and Just Right: It Depends on Where You Live." In *The Reference Shelf: Affordable Housing*, edited by Micah L. Issit, 71-74. Amenia, NY: Grey House Publishing, 2019.

MLA: Murray, Cecile, and Jenny Schuetz. "Housing in the US Is Too Expensive, and Just Right: It Depends on Where You Live." *The Reference Shelf: Affordable Housing*, edited by Micah L. Issit, Grey House Publishing, 2019, pp. 71-74.

APA: Murray, C., & J. Schuetz. (2019). Housing in the US is too expensive, and just right: It depends on where you live. In Micah L. Issit (Ed.), *The reference shelf: Affordable housing* (pp. 71-74). Amenia, NY: Grey House Publishing.

We Don't Need More Housing Projects

By Edgar Olsen

The Washington Post, October 11, 2016

The current system of low-income housing assistance is fertile ground for reform. The majority of housing assistance recipients are served by project-based programs whose cost is enormously excessive for the housing provided. But one major change would allow us to serve many more poor households without increasing public spending.

To serve the interests of taxpayers who want to help low-income families, Congress should shift the budget for low-income housing assistance away from supporting housing projects and toward helping tenants pay their rent. It should also eliminate subsidies for the construction of new housing projects. Phasing out housing projects to shore up the housing voucher program would ultimately free up the resources to provide housing assistance to millions of additional people.

Proponents of subsidizing the construction and operation of housing projects have launched a major lobbying effort to greatly expand the Low-Income Housing Tax Credit Program, one that has garnered support from influential lawmakers. They offer two main rationales: that it will help provide housing to people who are homeless and help low-income households that spend a high fraction of their income on housing. Neither objective justifies subsidizing the construction of housing projects.

Many poor households are not offered low-income housing assistance in the form of a voucher or a spot in a housing project, and many of these households spend high portions of their modest incomes on housing because they value more desirable neighborhoods, convenient locations and higher-quality homes more than other goods that must be sacrificed to live where they choose.

These households already have housing. We don't need to build new housing for them. If we think that their housing is unaffordable, the cheapest so-

> **The reason that people are homeless is not a shortage of units but lack of money to pay the rent for existing units.**

lution is for the government to pay a part of the rent, and the housing voucher program—the system's most cost-effective tool—does that. This program also ensures that its participants live in units that meet minimum standards.

Building new units is a much more expensive solution to the affordability problem. The best study of the Department of Housing and Urban Development's largest program subsidizing the construction of privately owned housing projects indicated an excess taxpayer cost of at least 72 percent compared with housing vouchers that provide equally good housing at the same cost to tenants. Publicly owned housing projects have an even larger excess cost.

Furthermore, it is not necessary or desirable to construct new units to house the homeless. In the entire country, there are only about 600,000 homeless people on a single night and more than 3 million vacant units available for rent. All homeless people could be easily accommodated in vacant existing units, which would be much less expensive than building new units for them. The reason that people are homeless is not a shortage of units but lack of money to pay the rent for existing units.

A housing voucher would solve that problem. A major HUD-funded random assignment experiment called the Family Options Study compared the cost and effectiveness of housing vouchers and subsidized housing projects for serving the homeless. Subsidized housing projects were far less effective and more than twice as expensive.

People who want to provide housing assistance to more of the poorest households should support expansion of the housing voucher program rather than subsidizing the construction of additional housing projects.

Print Citations

CMS: Olsen, Edgar. "We Don't Need More Housing Projects." In *The Reference Shelf: Affordable Housing*, edited by Micah L. Issit, 76-77. Amenia, NY: Grey House Publishing, 2019.

MLA: Olsen, Edgar. "We Don't Need More Housing Projects." *The Reference Shelf: Affordable Housing*, edited by Micah L. Issit, Grey House Publishing, 2019, pp. 76-77.

APA: Olsen, E. (2019). We don't need more housing projects. In Micah L. Issit (Ed.), *The reference shelf: Affordable housing* (pp. 76-77). Amenia, NY: Grey House Publishing.

The Affordable Housing Crisis

By Richard A. Epstein

Hoover Institution, February 27, 2017

Housing policy has become yet another flashpoint in these highly polarized times. Much of the controversy swirls around President Donald Trump's nomination of Ben Carson, a distinguished neurosurgeon, as Secretary of Housing and Urban Development. HUD operates a wide range of subsidized federal housing programs that impassioned critics of his nomination are sure Carson will dismember. His chief vice in their eyes is his lack of direct experience working in the housing area. In a real sense this is a mixed blessing. On the one hand, these programs must be managed—and, ideally, by someone competent and somewhat knowledgeable in the field. On the other, his greatest strength is that from an outside perspective he understands that many of these programs must be cut back or shut down. There is some overstatement in the charge that HUD is a socialist program. But there is much truth to the claim that many of its programs have seriously aggravated housing difficulties around the country, especially for the most vulnerable groups.

The key challenge is to choose the correct path for housing reform. Many of Carson's critics think the proper line is to require new developments to save a proportion of units for low-income residents, which will ensure, they claim, "that economically diverse neighborhoods and housing affordability will be preserved for generations to come." The implicit assumption behind this position is that government agents have enough information to organize complex social institutions, when in fact they are slow to respond to changes in market conditions and are often blissfully unaware of the many different strategies that are needed in different market settings. No one wants to say that governments should not lay out street grids and organize infrastructure. But they operate at a huge comparative disadvantage when it comes to real estate development on that public grid.

Far superior is an alternative view that I have long championed. The first thing to do is to abandon the assumption that there is a systematic market failure requiring government intervention. The second is to remove all barriers to entry in the housing markets, so that supply can increase and prices can fall. These barriers are numerous, and include an endless array of fees, taxes, and permits that grant vast discretionary authority to local officials. A removal of these burdens will allow us to harness the private knowledge of developers who will seek to work in those portions of the market that hold the greatest profit opportunities.

The critics often fear that developers will look to build only mansions and high-rise towers to satisfy the endless desires of the millionaire class. But that hyperbole ignores every relevant feature of an unregulated housing market. Most critically, as costs of housing construction and maintenance go down, developers are able to offer lower-priced units to people of more limited means. Prices are kept low by new entry across the full spectrum. Some developers will move quickly into the luxury market, but others, knowing of the potential glut, will move into other market niches in different neighborhoods where they can secure the highest rate of return. And once that is done, the expanded supply will provide more opportunities to lower-income tenants.

Yet as matters stand, there is good reason why developers gravitate to the higher end of today's highly regulated market—because they cannot absorb the high fixed costs of planning, permitting, and construction for smaller projects. As demand surges in highly desirable supply contracts, the result is always the same. Equilibrium prices march steadily upward, leading local activists to cry for a new round of subsidies, restrictions, and reforms, all of which start the cycle over again.

One highly controversial program is Measure S, which is on the ballot in Los Angeles. As the *Los Angeles Times*—a fierce opponent of this ballot initiative—notes, "Measure S would impose a two-year moratorium on all real estate projects that require a General Plan amendment, zone change or increase in allowable height." One LA project that would be forced to stop would house homeless veterans and other low-income folks. Nor should that consequence come as a surprise. The reference to amendments and zoning changes cuts far more deeply than it appears, because under modern land use law, modifications of existing ordinances, often called "contract zoning," are routinely necessary to get a deal through. The way it works is the initial zoning laws are set in a highly restrictive fashion. The developer then has to come forward with a package of benefits for the community as a way to secure a more favorable zoning classification. By blocking renegotiations, Measure S freezes everything, virtually assuring a mass developer exit from the market. The preexisting process already is a huge deterrent to development, which started its relentless decline after the 1950s with the onset of strict zoning regulations.

The bad ideas for housing regulation do not end with blanket moratoria. Indeed, the most popular approach nationwide does not directly limit the amount of new housing that can be built. Instead, it embraces "inclusive zoning" in which the developer is forced to set aside some fraction of the total number of units as designated affordable housing units. As one might expect, the worse the underlying situation, the more stringent the matching requirements. Thus, this past December, Portland, Oregon, unanimously approved its "Historic Inclusionary Housing Program" that requires all developments of twenty or more units to designate 20 percent of these units as affordable. Look for a lot of 19 unit projects. Earlier in the summer of 2016, San Francisco, whose zany housing policies have no known limitations, raised the ante when its voters approved Proposition C. Prior to its adoption, developers had three options: Set aside 12 percent of units for affordable housing; build some units off-site; or contribute to an "in lieu" fund to enable the City to take on new projects. Proposition C raises the ante by insisting that the projects have 25 percent on-site housing; 33 percent off-site housing; or that their developers pay a commensurately higher fee.

This program is reasonable insofar as it imposes less stiff requirements for the on-site units than the off-site ones. These are usually more expensive to construct. And, ironically, they are less desirable to low-income tenants who cannot afford to live in high-price areas. It is just for that reason that a recent op-ed in the *New York Times* by financial journalist Eric Uhlfelder called for a "new fix" for affordable housing that requires the imposition of an annual luxury tax "on new high-end condos and rentals." As Uhlfelder notes, this proposal essentially eliminates the difficulties of in-kind contributions. But it is hard to see why it should make a dent in the underlying supply problem. Generally speaking, the elimination of two options will not improve the position of the developers. Instead, it becomes absolutely critical to know which of these new construction projects will be covered by the luxury tax and which will not. If the line is announced in advance, a City will find itself in the odd position of insisting that new construction meets its parameters, as developers seek to gain permits under the radar. If the rate, moreover, is set incorrectly, the entire scheme could fail for want of takers, sending the city's program back to square one.

> The correct answer is to stop eminent domain abuse, to peel away layers of regulation, and to cut out the extensive network of government grants that impose strings on how housing can be built.

One way to avoid this difficulty, now under active consideration in Los Angeles, is for developers to pay a so-called "linkage fee" on all new commercial and residential housing, which can then be used to remedy the chronic undersupply of affordable housing. The program here, however, could—in combination with the city's new project moratoria—put all development into paralysis. One clear improvement over both the Uhlfelder and Los Angeles proposals is to sever the link between new affordable housing programs and any special tax on new real estate development, by funding all local affordable housing programs out of general revenues. That switch in emphasis means that a specific tax is less likely to wreck a specific segment of the housing industry. It will also provide a modest political check on the willingness of local governments to dedicate funds to affordable housing programs, given popular resistance to overall tax increases. That just might switch the political balance in favor of the liberalization of the notorious zoning codes that have stifled new construction in the first place.

But even these are really stopgap measures. All taxes deter development. Market liberalization increases it. Folks like Uhlfedler are explicit that they resort to these schemes because they expect a Trump administration to cut back on federal subsidies, which I regard as a welcome counterforce to unsound HUD programs. So it is back again to Ben Carson, whose real comparative advantage is that he has no historical connection with the dysfunctional public housing world. But Carson does grasp the dangers of "mandated social-engineering schemes," and appreciates the risks of "unintended consequences" of various social interventions. Hopefully, when he takes over HUD, he will bring with him a broom that will sweep clean much of the detritus that currently exists.

As Carson has noted, one of his first targets will be the multiple Obama programs that grant HUD funds to affordable housing that is built in wealthier neighborhoods. Apart from the endless paperwork these "fair housing" programs require, they also depart from Uhlfelder's observation that most local housing activists would prefer to use government grants to fix up housing in areas where low and moderate-income people actually choose to live. Any decision by Carson to scrap the rule would be a vast improvement for housing markets, as lower administrative costs would lead to higher levels of local development.

The so-called housing experts all sign on to the general mission of HUD to deal with the various ills of housing shortages, but none of them have the slightest interest in the market solutions that could improve the overall situation. To make the point more clearly, market solutions do not include letting developers steamroll small property owners through eminent domain abuse, or allowing local communities to pass restrictive zoning and permitting requirements that are intended to block low-income housing. Rather, the correct answer is to stop eminent domain abuse, to peel away layers of regulation, and to cut out the extensive network of government grants that impose strings on how housing can be built. Perhaps Carson does not know much about the current programs. But if he puts the necessary reforms in place, he will have no need to master the details of endless federal, state, and local regulations that have created the affordable housing crisis in the first place.

Print Citations

CMS: Epstein, Richard A. "The Affordable Housing Crisis." In *The Reference Shelf: Affordable Housing*, edited by Micah L. Issit, 78-81. Amenia, NY: Grey House Publishing, 2019.

MLA: Epstein, Richard A. "The Affordable Housing Crisis." *The Reference Shelf: Affordable Housing,* edited by Micah L. Issit, Grey House Publishing, 2019, pp. 78-81.

APA: Epstein, R.A. (2019). The affordable housing crisis. In Micah L. Issit (Ed.), *The reference shelf: Affordable housing* (pp. 78-81). Amenia, NY: Grey House Publishing.

Why Are We Relying on Tech Overlords Like Microsoft for Affordable Housing?

By Shaun Scott

The Guardian, January 22, 2019

Like many major metropolitan areas, Seattle is currently mired in what writer and housing activist Laura Bernstein has described as "a dual crisis of climate and affordability." A lack of affordable housing near industry has led to carbon-intensive sprawl – think of all those commuting cars – and economic distress among Seattleites. So, last Wednesday, when Microsoft announced a plan to dedicate $500m towards alleviating the affordable housing crisis in the area, one might have been forgiven for thinking it was an entirely good thing.

Indeed, the impact that $500m will make should not be understated. In the Puget Sound area, $250m of the funds will go towards the construction of housing that people making 60% of the area median income ($48,150 for a two-person household) can afford. Another $225m will help area developers complete projects that have stalled for lack of funding, and also acquire land for future projects. Microsoft will also be granting $25m to local homeless aid organizations and anti-eviction lawyers. The money also comes coupled with a suggestion that local governments relax regressive zoning restrictions that make building affordable apartments illegal in 75% of Seattle's city limits. In sum, this package will make a real material difference for Seattle's houseless, housing insecure and rent-burdened populations.

But when you look the Microsoft gift horse in the mouth, certain cavities are visible. For instance, $475m of the funds are not, as is widely assumed, donations. They're actually market-rate loans that affordable housing providers and government agencies will need to pay back. the *Seattle Times* reporter Mike Rosenberg notes that Microsoft will be turning a profit on this endeavor, while Seattle politics blog SCC Insight has cynically observed that the company is simply looking for places to sink some of its $135bn in liquid assets. In a declining stock market ransacked by Trump-induced economic insecurity, where better than an anemic public housing market to buy low and make a buck?

The bigger problem at hand is that this bucket of funds had to come from a billion-dollar company, and not local government, in the first place. Washington state has no income tax; if it had even a minuscule one, it could have raised many times more than $500m over a longer period of time. As it stands, for the state with the most regressive tax code in the nation, even a $500m windfall is too little; for the 191 King county residents who died homeless in 2018, it is tragically too late.

In May 2018, the Seattle city council introduced a modest tax on major corporations in the area; it repealed it a month later when the Seattle chamber of commerce spent nearly half a million dollars to excite rightwing opposition. Along with Amazon and Starbucks, Vulcan (Microsoft's satellite real estate enterprise) was one of the corporations that contributed to the anti-tax campaign. Seen in the light of this nasty political fight, the company's $500m gift seems a lot less like a donation, and more like a neoliberal rebrand.

In a political era defined by declining public investment, think back on all the basic services that America's tech overlords have attempted to recreate. The list is staggering. Silicon Valley transportation shuttles have caricatured public transportation. With its Prime Book Box subscription, Amazon has parodied public libraries. Tesla CEO Elon Musk has dropped $10m a mile on a kooky transit tunnel. And now, with its $500m contribution, Microsoft seeks to replace public housing. But the problem is that when we rely on capricious capitalists to do right by the public sector, they will always be a day late and a dollar short. The public sector can do better.

During capitalism's so-called "golden age," between the end of the second world war and the early 1970s, high corporate tax rates subsidized the social safety net and public housing. Today, major corporations like Microsoft stash profits in offshore tax shelters, well out of reach of governments in need of revenue to fund basic services. Here in rainy Seattle, many residents living under the cloud of Jeff Bezos-era techno-libertarianism believe that the best we can do is wait for wealth to trickle down.

With even modestly progressive redistributive taxes, we wouldn't have to depend on the kindness of oligarchs to house our citizens.

But to meet its affordable housing crisis, Seattle could raise $500m of its own money by issuing municipal bonds. With visionary leadership, the city could embark on radical neighborhood densification via comprehensive zoning reform. If adopted by all major American cities, such a measure would achieve half the carbon reductions needed to hold global temperatures to a rise of 2C (3.6F). And with even modestly progressive redistributive taxes, we wouldn't have to depend on the kindness of oligarchs to house our citizens.

We should thank Microsoft for the aid and wish it the best of luck turning a profit on its foray into philanthropy. But a cash-strapped public in desperate need of relief shouldn't allow software companies to have the final word.

Print Citations

CMS: Scott, Shaun. "Why Are We Relying on Tech Overlords Like Microsoft for Affordable Housing?" In *The Reference Shelf: Affordable Housing*, edited by Micah L. Issit, 82-84. Amenia, NY: Grey House Publishing, 2019.

MLA: Scott, Shaun. "Why Are We Relying on Tech Overlords Like Microsoft for Affordable Housing?" *The Reference Shelf: Affordable Housing*, edited by Micah L. Issit, Grey House Publishing, 2019, pp. 82-84.

APA: Scott, S. (2019). Why are we relying on tech overlords like Microsoft for affordable housing? In Micah L. Issit (Ed.), *The reference shelf: Affordable housing* (pp. 82-84). Amenia, NY: Grey House Publishing.

Everything You Wanted to Know about the Affordable Housing Debate

By Matthew Yglesias
Vox, May 11, 2015

What's Affordable Housing?

Housing policy is one of the main issues that local governments deal with. It encompasses several overlapping concerns. Making sure that everyone has a decent place to live is an important general priority. People are also interested in ensuring that economic diversity exists in specific cities, metropolitan areas, or neighborhoods. Last but not least, there is interest in maintaining specific communities and community ties without unduly displacing people.

Many regions have a shortage of affordable housing. The National Low Income Housing Coalition publishes a report annually showing the "housing wage" that a person would need to earn full time (40 hours a week, 52 weeks a year) in order for a two-bedroom rental unit to be affordable by the official government standard.

This housing wage is more than low-income workers typically make. And in some states, like California, the housing wage is very high. This problem is especially severe because on average the least-affordable cities are also the wealthiest ones, which means that a lack of affordable housing can lock people out of good job opportunities.

Policymakers have a variety of tools to address affordability-related concerns—rent control, inclusionary zoning ordinances, targeted subsidies—but economists generally agree that the only comprehensive way to lower prices is to increase the supply of houses, usually by changing zoning rules to become more friendly to new construction.

How Does the Government Define Affordable Housing?

The federal Department of Housing and Urban Development (HUD) defines an "affordable dwelling" as one that a household can obtain for 30 percent or less of its income. But this varies from city to city.

For example: a household is considered "low-income" if it makes less than 80 percent of the median income in the local area (this is called Area Median Income, or AMI). So, by this definition, a dwelling is considered "affordable" for low-income families if it costs less than 24 percent of the area median income.

Obviously these precise thresholds are a bit arbitrary. In the real world, spending 31 percent of your income on housing is not especially more burdensome than spending 29 percent, and different families are very differently situated in terms of child care expenses, health care expenses, and other necessities. But that's the official definition.

What's Wrong with the Official Definition of Affordable Housing?

One problem is that that many families try to reduce their housing costs by moving further away from job centers. But this simply increases their transportation costs—so a simple "affordable housing" metric might not capture the whole story. The Center for Neighborhood Technology offers a more holistic H+T Affordability Index that considers both housing and commuting costs.

Another problem is that the concept of Area Median Income (AMI) can exaggerate the affordability of housing in high-income areas. In the Washington, DC metropolitan area, for example, the median income is $107,500, which means that a family of three with an income of $48,375 is considered "low income" for housing affordability purposes. That means a unit could qualify as affordable for a low income family while still being well outside the price range of a family living near the poverty line.

The fact that many high-income households live in the DC area does not magically make mid-priced houses affordable to the city's actual low-income residents. By basing affordability metrics on the local median income, AMI implies that when housing affordability gets so dismal that lower income people leave, your city has actually increased the affordability of its housing stock. Since the highest income metro areas in America are often the least affordable, this is a substantial distortion.

How Can We Make Housing More Affordable?

There are two basic types of policies that could make a large difference in housing affordability:

- First, the government could directly give money or discounted housing to low-income families. Obviously a family that receives a free house can now afford housing. By the same token, families that receive more money can afford a wider range of houses.

- Second, policymakers could increase the number of dwellings in a given metropolitan area. This could be done either by relaxing restrictions on the size of buildings that can be built, or by relaxing restrictions that mandate minimum sizes of individual dwelling units. Cities tend to have a number of zoning rules that artificially restrict the supply of housing.

Governments and political activists are often very interested in using rent control or inclusionary zoning policies to address housing affordability issues. But those tools only redistribute a fixed supply of housing, and can't actually expand the number of people who can afford to dwell in a particular place.

Why Is Increasing Supply So Central to Affordability?

Any approach to housing affordability that ignores the supply side will ultimately run into a problem familiar from the children's game musical chairs—if there aren't enough homes to go around, someone has to lose out.

In an unregulated, unsubsidized market the people who lose out are going to be the people with the least money to spend. Various regulatory measures or subsidies can change that and provide targeted assistance to some households. But in many areas, the basic problem is that demand for housing is high. The technology boom has caused many people to want to live in Palo Alto, but there aren't enough houses to go around. The renewed fashionability of urban living means that many people want to live in Manhattan, but there aren't enough apartments to go around. For housing to be more affordable, the supply of houses needs to increase.

What Is Zoning?

The term "zoning" is often used loosely to refer to a broad set of regulations that govern the use of urban and suburban land. It is more strictly used to refer to what's also sometimes called "Euclidean zoning" (after the village of Euclid, Ohio not the Greek mathematician) which seeks to segregate different kinds of building uses from one another.

Under Euclidean zoning, a given patch of land is set aside for residential use, for office buildings, for shopping centers, for light industry, or whatever else. There are also "form-based" zoning codes that regulate the shape of buildings rather than the activities that take place inside them. Typically either a Euclidean or a form-based zoning code will distinguish between areas where multi-family apartment buildings are allowed and where they are banned.

Other kinds of regulations may or may not be considered zoning by particular jurisdictions. It is common, for example, to require certain minimum amounts of parking to be included with new construction projects, a rule that often de facto limits the amount of density that is allowed. Jurisdictions may also have rules about "lot occupancy" (how much space must be left unbuilt and reserved for yards) or the minimum size of lots. These regulations can all restrict the supply of housing in an area. If houses are legally required to be built on larger lots, fewer houses can be built in a given area.

How Does Rent Control Impact Housing Affordability?

At first blush, a "rent control" law that puts a ceiling on the amount of rent a landlord can charge should make housing more affordable. Economists often teach in Econ 101 that this is wrong, however. By making it less profitable to build new apartments, the argument goes, rent control laws perversely make housing less affordable by making it scarcer.

The Econ 101 argument is certainly possible in theory, but it is unlikely to be a significant factor in the contemporary United States. In the markets with the worst affordability problems, it's usually zoning rather than rent control that is restricting the supply of housing. Massachusetts, for example, entirely scrapped rent control in 1994. But that hasn't led to a surge of high-rise construction near Harvard Square—despite rising housing prices—for the simple reason that high-rise construction violates the zoning code.

What Is Inclusionary Zoning?

Inclusionary zoning (IZ) ordinances have become increasingly popular affordable housing measures in recent years.

The way inclusionary-zoning works is it requires that a certain share of units in new projects be set aside for families under a given income threshold (typically 80% of the Area Median Income) at a price that's affordable for such a family. This is an effective tool for maintaining economic diversity in a rapidly developing neighborhood, but its impact on the overall affordability of a city or a metropolitan area is ambiguous.

When IZ is used as part of a larger political process aimed at increasing the amount of construction that's allowed in a desirable area ("upzoning") it can be a very potent tool for affordability. But if IZ isn't paired with upzoning, it has an ambiguous impact on affordability. A small number of households will end up getting a home they couldn't otherwise afford. But everyone else will be left with a smaller pool of market rate units to bid on.

What Is Gentrification?

Different people mean different things by "gentrification," but typically it refers to a process by which higher-income people and retail outlets that cater to them move into a neighborhood previously dominated by low-income households, artsy Bohemian types, immigrants, people of color, or some combination of the above.

People may bemoan gentrification simply because change per se can be discomfiting (perhaps your favorite neighborhood bar has been replaced by a P.F. Chang's) but also because they worry that gentrification is a process whereby the original residents are displaced by market forces.

Research by Columbia University's Lance Freeman suggests that displacement is actually relatively rare. Residential turnover in urban neighborhoods is high, with people frequently moving out of any given neighborhood. In non-gentrifying neighborhoods, poor people move out and are replaced with other poor people. In gentrifying neighborhoods, poor people who move out are replaced with non-poor people. But Freeman found little impact of gentrification on the pace of churn. Still, even if displacement on the individual level is rare, there's no doubt that widespread occurrence of gentrification is often associated with citywide increases in housing costs and intensifying affordable housing problems.

What Is Filtering?

Filtering is in some sense the opposite of gentrification. As Thomas Bier of the Brookings Institution explains, as old structures age they generally "deteriorate, become obsolete,

> **Economists generally agree that the only comprehensive way to lower prices is to increase the supply of houses, usually by changing zoning rules to become more friendly to new construction.**

fall out of fashion, and 'filter down' in value." This is what Jane Jacobs had in mind when she wrote that "new ideas need old buildings." All else being equal, rent is cheaper in an old building than a state-of-the-art one, which makes old commercial buildings ideal for startups.

The same is true of residential housing. As long as new buildings are being regularly built, some share of older buildings will "filter" down market and become affordable for families with lower incomes.

Won't Unregulated Developers Just Produce Tons of Luxury Housing?

This is unlikely. If you were to only build one building, you might well want to make it a high-priced, high-margin luxury project. But there are only so many millionaires in the country. As the number of projects increases, developers need to reach further down the market to reach a larger base of customers.

Think about car companies. Most auto firms do try to sell high-margin luxury vehicles. But they also make plenty of ordinary vehicles for middle-class car buyers, because there are only so many rich people to sell cars to. If you forced Toyota to only build a handful of cars per year, they would probably try to make them Lexuses rather than Corollas. But in an unconstrained market, Corollas predominate.

What's more, even luxury projects help address housing scarcity. In a marketplace with no new luxury projects, rich people don't forget that they enjoy fancy houses in appealing neighborhoods. They simply snap up older properties and renovate them (or house-flippers do it), thus blocking the process of filtering and taking middle-class residences off the market.

Whatever Happened to Public Housing?

The economic calamity of the Great Depression tended to restrain new construction activity in the 1930s. Then during World War II, there was a broad ban on civilian construction to ensure that resources were available for military use and war production. Consequently, the postwar United States faced a serious housing shortfall. This was addressed in many places with government-financed construction projects to build government-owned housing.

As the economic situation normalized, these public housing projects became concentrated clusters of housing for poor families. Then the general suburbanization trends and urban population decline of the 1960s, 70s, and 80s left the projects more isolated from jobs and economic activity. Rising crime (and plain old racism) led middle-class neighborhoods and suburbs to reject the idea of new public housing projects, further entrenching the nexus between public housing and ghettoization.

Over the past two decades, housing policy trends have been toward reducing the amount of public housing. Instead of spending money on public housing construction, funds tend to be spent on Section 8 housing assistance vouchers or on programs to reconfigure old public housing projects as mixed-income ones.

What Is Section 8?

The Housing Choice Voucher Program is laid out in Section 8 of the repeatedly amended Housing Act of 1937, and thus "Section 8" has become housing wonks' shorthand for the program. The idea of Section 8 is relatively simple: instead of money being spent to build public housing, the money is given to families as vouchers that cover part or all of the cost of renting from a private landlord.

The conceptual advantages of Section 8 are considerable. Most notably, it lets poor families decide for themselves what tradeoffs they want to make around building quality, location, price, and all the other relevant factors.

But there are also several problems. One is funding. Due to Congress's reluctance to appropriate large sums of money for housing assistance, the number of families who meet the eligibility criteria generally far exceeds the number of vouchers actually available. That leads to long waiting lists for families seeking help. Another is that landlords often prefer not to rent to Section 8 tenants, recreating the social isolation dynamic of public housing projects that Section 8 is supposed to mitigate.

What Is Exclusionary Zoning?

Exclusionary zoning is a process by which a neighborhood or town makes it de facto illegal for low-income—or at times even non-poor—people to live in a given area. The most blunt form is something like a ban on trailer parks or mobile homes.

More subtle forms of exclusionary zoning are also available. In Washington, DC's Spring Valley neighborhood, for example, homes must be located on lots that are at least 7,500 square feet. Minimum lot size rules are extremely common in America's suburbs, as are bans on multi-family structures. These kinds of measures, whether deliberately or unintentionally, make it impossible to locate cheap housing in the areas where it's applied.

Requirements that housing units include off-street parking can also serve as a form of exclusion, as carless households are disproportionately low-income.

If High-Density Zoning Is So Great, Why Are Manhattan and San Francisco So Expensive?

It is true that the densest county in America, Manhattan, is not exactly cheap. Nor is San Francisco, the second-densest city in the county. But the right question to ask is how much more expensive would these places be with less density. Suppose every apartment building on Fifth Avenue and Central Park West were reduced in height by 20 percent. Rich people would still like park views. But all that rich-person money would be chasing fewer units. Prices would rise. And the rich people who got priced out of Fifth Avenue would fan out across the city raising prices elsewhere.

Conversely, if San Francisco were allowed to be built up to New York City levels of density it could fit another 1.2 million people. Upzoning expensive Bay Area sub-urbs in San Mateo and Santa Clara counties could be even more beneficial.

If We Allow Denser Bulding, Isn't Everything Going to Get Too Crowded?

For starters, there are only so many people to go around. If rezoning were to cause some cities to become more crowded, it stands to reason that some other place is becoming less crowded. Different people will have different preferences about levels of crowding and will choose to live in different neighborhoods or different metropolitan areas.

More broadly, the fact that many people don't like too much crowding is pre-cisely why we don't need to worry too much about prescriptive residential land use rules. There is no reason to build a dense parcel unless someone wants to rent or buy it.

Print Citations

CMS: Yglesias, Matthew. "Everything You Wanted to Know about the Affordable Housing Debate." In *The Reference Shelf: Affordable Housing*, edited by Micah L. Issit, 85-91. Amenia, NY: Grey House Publishing, 2019.

MLA: Yglesias, Matthew. "Everything You Wanted to Know about the Affordable Housing Debate." *The Reference Shelf: Affordable Housing*, edited by Micah L. Issit, Grey House Publishing, 2019, pp. 85-91.

APA: Yglesias, M. (2019). Everything you wanted to know about the affordable housing debate. In Micah L. Issit (Ed.), *The reference shelf: Affordable housing* (pp. 85-91). Amenia, NY: Grey House Publishing.

It Can Cost $750,000 to Build an Affordable Housing Unit in California: Here's Why

By Laura Kusisto

The Wall Street Journal, September 21, 2018

A single unit of housing for a low-income family can cost nearly $750,000 to build in California, according to a government report that provides new details on the cost to taxpayers of building affordable housing in states with high land prices and heavy land-use regulations.

A new report from the Government Accountability Office highlights stark disparities in the cost to build affordable housing that qualifies for tax credits between states like California, which has more land-use regulations, and Texas, where it is much easier to get approval to build. A typical unit for a low-income family in San Francisco and Los Angeles costs around $400,000 to build. In Texas, where land-use regulations are much looser, the cost is about a third of that.

Median costs in Chicago and New York City were also high, at $315,000 and $282,000 respectively, the GAO found.

The investigation into the efficiency and effectiveness of the tax-credit program was conducted at the request of Chuck Grassley, chairman of the U.S. Senate's committee on the judiciary. The program, which allows investors to take federal tax credits in exchange for providing equity for affordable housing projects, represented roughly $8.4 billion of foregone revenue in 2017.

High construction costs limit the number of projects that can be built, by requiring states to allocate more tax credits to individual projects or to find other sources of funding to make projects work.

Land-use regulations are creating a stark divide between places that are adding housing quickly and remaining affordable to middle-income families, and places that are not. The new government report looks at projects that are stripped of most of the bells and whistles—from

> **High construction costs limit the number of projects that can be built, by requiring states to allocate more tax credits to individual projects or to find other sources of funding to make projects work.**

pet spas to marble countertops—that can drive up the cost of luxury projects. It focuses on rent-restricted housing targeted at families earning less than 80% of the local median income that qualifies for the tax credits.

The report has been anticipated among low-income housing developers and lobbyists, fearful it could tarnish a program that enjoys strong bipartisan support. In the end, the investigation revealed no single scandal but rather widespread challenges as construction and land costs soar in costly coastal markets, making it more difficult to build not only rentals that benefit from government tax credits but any moderately priced housing.

"It's not a good business model when the numbers are this high," said Rick Holliday, a developer and modular-construction factory owner in San Francisco. "We've got a lot of work to do because the costs in California are way out of whack."

Mr. Holliday said, for example, that he is building a homeless-housing project in Oakland where there is a $12,000 fee just to hook up water to each of the units.

Land costs helped drive the expense of building in California, according to the GAO, though the report didn't break out the factors that distinguish a typical $400,000 unit from one on the high end near $750,000. Daniel Garcia-Diaz, director of financial markets and community investments at the GAO, said government officials and developers also make decisions to promote certain social goals that ultimately end up driving up costs.

Those can include building projects in more expensive neighborhoods that offer residents better schools and job opportunities, building near transit, imposing certain green requirements, or demanding developers use local labor.

"The state really needs to monitor costs closely and realize the tradeoffs of having to spend more for a project," Mr. Garcia-Diaz said.

A recent report from the National Council of State Housing Agencies, a nonprofit lobby group for state affordable housing agencies, found similar disparities between the costs to build affordable housing in different states.

"So much of what is going into development costs and what is driving affordability challenges has to do with a set of costs and cost drivers that are local in nature," said Stockton Williams, the group's executive director.

Mr. Williams said those costs include everything from "not in my backyard" opposition to development to "burdensome regulations."

Print Citations

CMS: Kusisto, Laura. "It Can Cost $750,000 to Build an Affordable Housing Unit in California: Here's Why." In *The Reference Shelf: Affordable Housing*, edited by Micah L. Issit, 92-93. Amenia, NY: Grey House Publishing, 2019.

MLA: Kusisto, Laura. "It Can Cost $750,000 to Build an Affordable Housing Unit in California: Here's Why." *The Reference Shelf: Affordable Housing*, edited by Micah L. Issit, Grey House Publishing, 2019, pp. 92-93.

APA: Kusisto, L. (2019). It can cost $750,000 to build an affordable housing unit in California: Here's why. In Micah L. Issit (Ed.), *The reference shelf: Affordable housing* (pp. 92-93). Amenia, NY: Grey House Publishing.

President Trump Calls for Drastic Cuts to Affordable Housing

National Low Income Housing Coalition, February 12, 2018

President Donald Trump's Fiscal Year 2019 budget request—released today—proposes drastic cuts to housing benefits that help millions of low income seniors, people with disabilities, families with children, veterans, and other vulnerable people afford their homes. The proposal—unveiled less than two months after the president signed into law $1.5 trillion in tax cuts for wealthy individuals and corporations—would take away housing benefits from the lowest income people by slashing federal investments in affordable homes, increasing rents, and imposing harmful work requirements on America's struggling families. If enacted, it could leave even more low income people without an affordable home, undermining family stability, increasing evictions, and leading to more homelessness.

NLIHC strongly urges Congress to not only reject Mr. Trump's budget, but to significantly expand the investments in affordable homes that America's families and communities need to thrive. For more detailed information on the proposed budget cuts, see NLIHC's updated budget chart.

Overall, the Administration proposes to cut HUD by an astounding $8.8 billion or 18.3-percent compared to the 2017 enacted levels. In an addendum stemming from the bipartisan budget agreement, the president suggests that $2 billion above his request could be added back in for a final proposed cut of $6.8 billion.

At a time when the affordable housing crisis has reached new heights, and homelessness is increasing in some communities, the president proposes to eliminate essential housing and community development programs, like the national Housing Trust Fund, Community Development Block Grants, the HOME Investments Partnership Program, and the U.S. Interagency Council on Homelessness. The backlog of public housing capital repair needs is upwards of $40 billion, but the Administration proposes to entirely eliminate federal funding for capital repairs and slash funding to operate public housing.

The president would underfund rental assistance through the Housing Choice Voucher program by nearly $3 billion. While the administration suggests that additional funding provided in an addendum would avoid some of this impact, NLIHC still estimates that these cuts could lead to at least 200,000 housing vouchers being lost—a move that would increase homelessness and housing poverty.

The budget would also impose punitive measures that would jeopardize family stability, increasing the financial burdens they face through higher rents and harmful work requirements that often pushes families deeper into poverty. HUD suggests that it will send its proposal to cut housing benefits through rent increases and work requirements to Congress in March, however, we expect it will be substantially similar to draft legislation that was leaked in recent weeks. Learn more about President Trump's draft legislation to cut housing benefits, how cutting housing benefits would increase homelessness and housing poverty, and how it impacts your state.

"The breadth and depth of cruelty reflected in this budget proposal is breathtaking," says Diane Yentel, NLIHC president and CEO. "President Trump is making clear, in no uncertain terms, his willingness to increase evictions and homelessness—the families who could lose their rental assistance through severe funding cuts and for the low income and vulnerable seniors, people with disabilities and families with kids who will be unable to manage having to spend more of their very limited income to cover rent hikes. The Administration callously disregards its responsibility to the millions of households living in deteriorating public housing and to low income people and communities working to recover and rebuild after disasters by eliminating critical resources for public housing, rental housing construction, and community development. It's a cruel and unconscionable budget proposal and it should be soundly rejected by Congress."

HUD Programs

Rent Increases and Work Requirements Will Increase Homelessness and Housing Poverty

The budget supports cutting housing benefits for some of America's lowest income people by increasing rents and imposing work requirements on current and future tenants. While HUD plans to send its proposal to cut housing benefits to Congress in March, we expect it will be substantially similar to draft legislation that was leaked in recent weeks.

The proposed changes would hurt tenants already scraping to get by and would make it more difficult for them to achieve financial stability and live with dignity. The draft legislation proposes to increase rents on most non-elderly, non-disabled families by requiring that they pay 35% of their gross income, compared to 30% of their adjusted income. The very poorest elderly and disabled families would also see their rent increase up to 30% of their gross income or $50, whichever is higher. His proposal would eliminate income deductions for medical or childcare expenses for all households, primarily impacting seniors, people with disabilities, and families with children. It sets a new mandatory minimum rent for households assumed to be able to work at more than $150—or three times more than its current rate. And, the proposal allows housing providers to broadly impose work requirements, without any resources to help people gain the skills they need for well-paying jobs.

In an addendum, the White House suggests providing an additional $1 billion, stemming from the recent budget agreement, to avoid rent increases on elderly and disabled families in FY 2019. There is no assurance that funding will be allocated this way or that such protection will be afforded to these households in future years.

Taking away housing benefits from poor families will only force them to make impossible tradeoffs between paying rent or paying for medicine, groceries, and other necessities. Learn more about President Trump's draft legislation to cut housing benefits, how cutting housing benefits would increase homelessness and housing poverty, and how it impacts your state.

National Housing Trust Fund

Mr. Trump's budget calls for eliminating the national Housing Trust Fund (HTF), the first new housing resource that is exclusively targeted to help build and preserve housing affordable to people with the lowest incomes, including those experiencing homelessness.

NLIHC and a broad coalition of national, state, and local organizations are working to expand the HTF, which is funded through a small fee on Fannie Mae and Freddie Mac, through housing finance reform and other legislative opportunities. The president's proposal to eliminate the HTF could make it more difficult for housing finance reform legislation to attract the bipartisan support needed for passage.

Tenant-Based Rental Assistance

Mr. Trump would slash funding for tenant-based rental assistance (TBRA). The request provides $19.315 billion for TBRA. This includes $17.514 billion to renew previous contracts, or more than $3 billion less than what is needed to ensure that all contracts are fully renewed. As a result, NLIHC and others estimate that more than 330,000 vouchers would be lost.

The administration would also cut funding for new Section 811 mainstream vouchers for people with disabilities by $13 million and would zero out funding for new Family Unification and HUD-Veterans Affairs Supportive Housing (VASH) vouchers. The proposal does provide $4 million for HUD-VASH vouchers targeted to Native Americans, $3 million below the FY17 enacted level. The budget would reduce the amount of funds public housing authorities (PHAs) receive to administer the voucher program by 6% compared to FY17 funding levels.

The budget provides the HUD secretary with the authority to waive or specify alternative statutory and regulatory requirements under the voucher program, including those related to setting and adjusting allowable rents, payment standards, tenant rent contributions, occupancy standards, PHA program assessments, and PHA administrative, planning, and reporting requirements, if the HUD secretary finds that these would reduce costs or improve effectiveness.

In an addendum, the White House suggests providing an additional $700 million stemming from the recent budget agreement to restore 200,000 housing vouchers, reversing the administration's policy of recapturing vouchers during normal turn-over. It is unclear, however, whether the funding would be used this way.

Project-Based Rental Housing

The budget proposal would provide $10.866 billion to renew project-based rental assistance (PBRA) contracts for calendar year 2019, an increase of $50 million from the FY17 funding level. This amount would be insufficient to cover all existing contracts, considering both the House and Senate provide over $11 billion to renew PBRA contracts in their FY18 THUD spending bills.

Public Housing

Public housing takes a huge hit under the Trump budget proposal. The public housing capital fund, which received $1.942 billion in FY17, would be eliminated in FY19. The allocation for the operating fund would fall significantly from $4.4 billion in FY17 to $2.84 billion.

Instead, the administration requests $100 million for the Rental Assistance Demonstration (RAD) to convert more public housing into housing vouchers and PBRA, despite the fact that the ability to successfully convert public housing through RAD requires fully funding vouchers and PBRA. The request eliminates the sunset date for the RAD and removes the 225,000-unit cap on public housing conversions. It also expands RAD to Section 202 Housing for the Elderly Project Rental Assistance Contracts (PRAC).

The president proposes two new set-asides, including $30 million for competitive grants to facilitate the demolition of physically obsolete public housing properties and $300 million to support those PHAs that become finally insolvent due to the budget cuts. An additional $300 million—stemming from the recent budget agreement and provided through an addendum—could push the total set aside for insolvent PHAs to $600 million.

> **Taking away housing benefits from poor families will only force them to make impossible tradeoffs paying rent or paying for medicine, groceries, and other necessities.**

The administration also proposes "releasing certain housing assets to local control" and "a strategic reduction of the Public Housing portfolio." The budget claims that current tenants will continue to receive assistance, but it is unclear how the federal government could ensure this, given the changes it is proposing.

The president proposes allowing the HUD Secretary to not require or enforce the Physical Needs Assessment for public housing units.

The budget provides the HUD secretary with the authority to waive or set alternative statutory and regulatory requirements for PHAs, including administrative, planning, and reporting requirements, energy audits, income re-certifications, and program assessments, if the HUD secretary finds these would reduce costs or improve effectiveness.

Moreover, PHAs would be given the authority to comingle funding from the public housing operating and capital funds. Such authorization would allow PHAs to direct operating funds, which are used to provide tenants with homes, to cover the cost of repairs and rehabilitation.

Homelessness

Mr. Trump would maintain funding for homeless assistance programs at $2.38 billion, level to 2017 enacted levels. However, this amount is $73 million less than the amount the Senate would provide in its FY18 THUD spending bill.

Healthy Homes

The administration would provide flat funding for the Office of Lead Hazard Control and Healthy Homes grants, when compared to FY17.

Fair Housing

The budget would decrease funding for HUD's Office of Fair Housing and Equal Opportunity. Specifically, the Fair Housing Initiatives Program (FHIP) would be cut by $3 million.

Other HUD Programs

The budget would eliminate the Community Development Block Grant program, the HOME Investment Partnerships program, Choice Neighborhoods grants, the Section 4 Capacity Building program, and the Self-Help Homeownership Opportunity Program. There is no discussion of how eliminating CDBG would impact future disaster relief efforts, which heavily rely on CDBG-Disaster Recovery funds to address unmet housing and infrastructure needs.

The budget provides $563 million to the Section 202 Housing for the Elderly program, a $61 million increase from last year's funding level, but $10 million below the amount included in the House and Senate THUD spending bills. It also reduces funding for the Section 811 Housing for People with Disabilities program to $132 million, $14 million less than the FY17 level. The president proposes giving the HUD secretary the authority to not provide rent adjustments for properties under Section 202 and 811. This could make it more financially difficult to operate these properties. The budget would also allow Section 202 Project Rental Assistance Contract (PRAC) properties to convert under RAD.

Funding for the Housing Opportunities for People with AIDS (HOPWA) program would decrease to $330 million, down from $356 million in FY17.

The budget cuts funding for the Native American Housing Block Grant program by $54 million, or a little more than 8%, when compared to FY17. The Native Hawaiian Housing Block Grant program would receive no funds.

The administration is also requesting money to evaluate EnVision Centers, HUD Secretary Ben Carson's new initiative to establish privately funded community centers that offer supportive services focusing on economic empowerment, educational advancement, health and wellness, and character and leadership.

USDA Rural Housing

President Trump proposes to essentially eliminate all rural housing grants and direct loan programs at the Department of Agriculture (USDA). The budget would fund Section 521 Rural Rental Assistance at $1.37 billion, including $20 million for vouchers for residents in properties subject to prepayment. It is unclear whether this is sufficient to cover all existing contracts. In addition, the budget proposes increasing the minimum monthly rent for tenants living in Section 514 or Section 515 properties to $50.

The budget also eliminates funding for the Multifamily Preservation and Revitalization demonstration, Section 502 Direct Homeownership Loans, Section 514/516 Farm Worker Housing Loans and Grants, Section 523 Mutual and Self-Help Housing, and Section 504 Rural Housing Assistance grants.

The only housing programs that would remain—other than rental assistance—are guaranteed loan programs that use fees to offset any federal costs and tend to serve relatively higher income households.

Other Agencies

Mr. Trump would also:

Cut health and nutrition benefits by imposing work requirements on Medicaid recipients and new restrictions on the Supplemental Nutrition Assistance Program.

Eliminate funding for the U.S. Interagency Council on Homelessness, the Neighborhood Reinvestment Corporation (NeighborWorks America), and the Legal Services Corporation (Legal Aid), which is often the only resource available to help deeply low income people avoid unwarranted evictions.

Eliminate funding to the Treasury Department for Community Development Financial Institutions (CDFI) Fund grants and direct loans.

Eliminate the Low Income Home Energy Assistance Program (LIHEAP) and Community Services Block Grants (CSBG) at the Department of Health and Human Services.

Eliminate the Weatherization Assistance Program (WAP) at the Department of Energy.

Infrastructure Spending

President Trump's FY19 spending bill calls for a $200 billion infrastructure package that fails to include any new resources to address our nation's shortage of affordable rental homes and could divert existing resources to other purposes. Moreover, this one-time spending proposal would be paid for with cuts to existing programs that are funded annually through the appropriation process. This puts America's long-term investments in infrastructure at risk.

The plan includes increasing state volume caps on tax-exempt private activity bonds, which are used to finance the 4% Low Income Housing Tax Credit. Because the plan also expands the allowable use of bonds to all governmental infrastructure projects, however, this could ultimately reduce the availability of housing bonds to build and preserve affordable rental homes.

Overall, the infrastructure plan includes $100 billion as gap financing in state-funded projects, $50 billion in block grants to rural state governors, and $50 billion in "transformative" projects, expanded federal loans for transportation, rail, and drinking water and wastewater projects, and a capital financing fund for federal buildings. In addition to the spending components, the proposal calls for streamlining federal permitting decisions to be handled by a single federal agency.

NLIHC believes that housing is infrastructure and that affordable housing investments must be expanded—not reduced—in any infrastructure package.

It is unclear whether there is enough support to enact a broad infrastructure package in Congress. Some conservative Republicans disapprove of the price tag, while Democrats have voiced concern that the direct federal investment does not provide enough resources to address America's crumbling infrastructure.

Print Citations

CMS: "President Trump Calls for Drastic Cuts to Affordable Housing." In *The Reference Shelf: Affordable Housing*, edited by Micah L. Issit, 94-100. Amenia, NY: Grey House Publishing, 2019.

MLA: "President Trump Calls for Drastic Cuts to Affordable Housing." *The Reference Shelf: Affordable Housing*, edited by Micah L. Issit, Grey House Publishing, 2019, pp. 94-100.

APA: National Low Income Housing Coalition. (2019). President Trump calls for drastic cuts to affordable housing. (2019). In Micah L. Issit (Ed.), *The reference shelf: Affordable housing* (pp. 94-100). Amenia, NY: Grey House Publishing.

4
Housing and Welfare

By The Blackbird (Jay Black), via Wikimedia.

A homeless man sleeping on the street, something anti-homeless legislation tries to regulate. Laws criminalizing homelessness—restricting public areas in which sitting or sleeping are allowed, prohibiting begging, requiring people to go to shelters, dismantling "tent cities"—have been enforced in many parts of the States in an attempt to regulate the homelessness problem. Critics of this approach point out that a viable alternative to living on the streets must be put in place first.

Homelessness, Racial Disparity, and Long Commutes

At its heart, affordable housing is a social welfare issue. The central question is whether or not a society has a responsibility to control the evolution of the real estate and rental markets to ensure that quality housing is available to the greatest possible number of people. Decisions made by politicians, citizens, and industry leaders with regard to housing policies directly impact many social welfare issues, including homelessness, poverty rates, and racial equality.

Homelessness in the United States

There have always been some Americans who are dismissive about homelessness and poverty or who see these issues as reflections of some kind of "social Darwinism," a now largely defunct group of theories that emerged in the 1800s and were used to argue that those who failed to achieve in society were less able, intelligent, or skilled. Arguments in this vein were used by conservatives at the turn of the last century to argue against social reforms and government intervention to address poverty and homelessness, and echoes of this basic attitude can still be found in discussions of homelessness and poverty in the twenty-first century. In the intervening years, research has demonstrated, conclusively, that achievement in the United States is not directly correlated with skill, effort, or intelligence, but is heavily influenced by familial or other support and, in general, one's starting point in the socioeconomic spectrum.

The perception that homelessness can be solved by giving homeless people jobs is incorrect and derives from an oversimplification of the homelessness problem. The Urban Institute released a study in 2018 indicating that approximately 25 percent of the U.S. homeless population are already employed. The National Coalition for the Homeless has determined that 40 to 60 percent of homeless people move in and out of full-time or part-time work and yet most are unable to earn sufficient wages to break the cycle of homelessness. What's more, research indicates that the population of working homeless people and families is growing, as wage growth has been stagnant and insufficient to enable many Americans to keep pace with the increasing cost of living. The National Low Income Housing Coalition estimates that, on average, a renter in America needs a wage of around $21.00 per hour to afford a two-bedroom apartment. However, the federal minimum wage is $7.25 and the average wage for hourly workers is $16.38, meaning that for many, even basic accommodations appropriate for a family may be out of reach.[1]

According to the Department of Housing and Urban Development, affordable housing is housing that costs no more than 30 percent of a person's income. Those who pay more than this proportion of their income are vulnerable to economic turmoil and less able to weather emergent financial pressures, such as a medical crisis, pregnancy, or interruptions in employment. Though some might imagine that catastrophic events are necessary to precipitate homelessness, this is not the case. A medical or family emergency, stock market fluctuations, or a temporary loss in employment can result in poverty and homelessness for individuals at many levels of the income spectrum. How well a person or family is buttressed against these outcomes depends on education level, field of employment, job security, region, fluctuations in pay rates for various industries, and the presence or absence of family or other support networks.

Obtaining a college or higher-level degree can provide advantages in job security and access to higher pay and so can reduce the risk of financial insecurity. However, the cost of higher education has risen to such a degree that many without family assets to help defray the cost find themselves trapped between education debt and the possibility of unstable employment. Some take on this debt only to experience difficulties in paying it back, potentially resulting in damaged credit and other financial difficulties. In some parts of the country, even college-educated, skilled workers struggle to earn enough to live affordably and remain vulnerable to economic hardship even after following the generally accepted path to security and success.

For those without a college education, real wages have changed little over the last 40 years even as the cost of living has increased. Further, although corporate profits have risen significantly over the past 50 years, corporations, in many cases, have not distributed this increased wealth within their companies. Since the 1970s, productivity in America has increased by 77 percent while hourly pay has grown by only 12 percent. This simple equation shows that Americans are now working harder than ever, for a smaller share of the profit. As Matthew Desmond wrote in a *New York Times* article on the issue, "American workers are being shut out of the profits they are helping to generate. . . . Today, 41.7 million laborers—nearly a third of the American work force—earn less than $12 an hour, and almost none of their employers offer health insurance."[2]

In some of America's most expensive regions, like much of the state of California, even individuals holding college degrees who work in jobs that would qualify as lucrative in other parts of the country can struggle to afford even basic rental properties and household expenses. While some might suggest that those who cannot afford to live comfortably in places like California should move to parts of the country where their skills would translate into more financial gain, this is easier said than done. For some, there may be family barriers to leaving an overpriced region. For others, jobs in a particular field might only be available in areas that also feature high housing and other costs. Increasingly, in America's most productive economic centers, workers in both labor and skilled fields migrate from areas with more affordable housing or rental rates to suburban or urban centers where they can find work. The need to commute long distances creates additional expenses and reduces the benefit of even advanced employment. Factor in the costs of having a family and the need to facilitate an entire family's commute for education, health care, and other purposes, and families at many levels of the income spectrum can struggle to remain financially stable.[3]

After seven years of overall decline in homelessness in the United States, 2017 and 2018 saw the homelessness rate rising in America, dramatically in some states. Between 2007 and 2017, North Dakota saw the single greatest increase, with a rise in homelessness of nearly 71.2 percent, while South Dakota and Wyoming each saw more than 60 percent growth. In Washington, DC, the nation's capital, nearly 1 percent of residents were homeless in 2018.[4] Many advocates for affordable housing reform argue that the solution to homelessness has already been determined; and that is to create more affordable housing. Professor Margot Kushel of the University of California San Francisco, a lead researcher on homelessness, told Wired in 2018, "This is not something like pancreatic cancer, where thousands of scientists are striving to find a solution for a really difficult problem that we literally don't know what to do about. We actually know what to do. We just lack the will."

Beyond housing, there is another layer to combating homelessness: integrating individuals back into communities. Writing in CityLab in 2018, Michael Rowe and Charles Barber describe a program in New Haven, Connecticut, where the goal is not only to help individuals find homes, but also to begin seeing themselves as connected to their community and as citizens with a role to play in society. This effort touches on deeper aspect of America's homelessness and poverty, that individuals already facing the burdens of poverty and homelessness also exist within a culture that delegitimizes the challenges they face.[5]

The Discrimination Dimension

Since the 1960s, the United States has made considerable progress in combating housing discrimination, which can be defined as professional, economic, and other practices that result in discrimination against members of certain groups when it comes to housing accessibility or affordability. In the 1930s, the US federal government had embraced systematic racial prejudice to the extent that the government refused to back home loans in areas with predominantly black populations. It took the Civil Rights Movement of the 1950s and 60s to change this practice and to create fair housing laws that are supposed to protect against discrimination in housing or financing. However, prejudice still plays a role in housing outcomes. As recently as 2013 a study from the Department of Housing and Urban Development (HUD), partnered with the Urban Institute in Washington DC, conducted studies using "pair testing" in which individuals with equal qualifications (one white and the other a person of color) engaged in the process of inquiring about rentals or home buying opportunity. The study indicated significantly different outcomes. White customers were provided with more options and offered lower rental prices than POC applicants with similar or better qualifications.[6]

In 2018, Urban Institute studies indicated that while progress had been made in combating discrimination, America had not eliminated the issue. After years of gains, between 2000 and 2015 black homeownership rates fell to 41.2 percent. This means, essentially, that black homeownership rates are as low in 2018 as they were before the 1968 Fair Housing Law prohibited racial discrimination in real estate practices. Studies of the drop in homeownership among black families indicates that it is related to the 2007-2010 financial recession. The additional barriers facing black families and individuals who lost their homes during the recession has essentially meant that these individuals have had a more difficult time trying to climb back to homeownership in comparison to white individuals and families, at similar income levels, who also saw financial hardship and loss of living conditions during the recession.[7]

It is also important to understand that the racial, class, and gender discrimination that was common in real estate in the 1950s and '60s still impacts patterns of property ownership and regional economic outcomes. In the 1960s, when black families were functionally shut out of home ownership in some of the nation's most economically prolific regions, a pattern was created that continues to impact outcomes today. These prejudicial policies and corporate behavior created many of the neighborhoods and communities that exist today. For instance, parts of Oakland were classified by the Federal Housing Administration as "C" in the 1960s, meaning that ownership was restricted to white persons. Even after such federal policies were prohibited, the patterns of occupancy and ownership that were created under the discriminatory patterns of the past have a generational impact on the economic outcomes of persons living in the present. For black families in the 1960s, the only available option for home ownership in many areas was to purchase properties in already economically impoverished neighborhoods where lower property taxes meant fewer amenities and underfunded education systems. Generation after generation, the legacy of racially motivated policies disadvantages individuals by reducing the level of familial, generational, educational, and community support available to some individuals and families. Racial policies, even if now prohibited, reverberate into the present, and, coupled with existing prejudice, have an important impact on economic indicators of stability, such as employment and property ownership.[8]

It is also important recognize that discrimination in housing is not simply a racial issue. Individuals in low-income brackets also face discrimination, in the form of direct and indirect measures used to prevent their occupying more productive areas where employment and amenities might help to achieve better outcomes. Individuals with physical and mental handicaps face prejudice and disadvantages when participating in either the rental or property ownership industries. In the modern era, with prejudice against Muslim individuals and individuals of Middle Eastern decent peaking in the United States, individuals in these groups are facing increased prejudice and exclusion from both job and property markets. Lesbian, Gay, Bisexual, Transgender, and Queer (LGBTQ) renters and potential property buyers have, in many cases, also experienced prejudicial treatment when attempting to enter the market.

Discrimination and prejudice are as much part of America's present as they are part of the nation's turbulent past and both the historic and contemporary manifestations of discrimination impact outcomes for millions of Americans. Home ownership has long been touted as one of the most important activities for building personal financial stability but, even when ownership is not available, acceptable rental property is a keystone to familial and personal stability and advancement. Affordable housing is a social welfare issue because, for many, housing is the basis of psychological and physical safety, security, and stability. This is why some advocates believe that access to affordable housing should be seen as a basic human right. If the goal of economic reform and policy is to get as many Americans as possible working and advancing towards prosperity, then affordable housing is an essential factor.

Micah L. Issitt

Works Used

Daugherty, Owen. "Homelessness Rates Increase for Second Straight Year." *The Hill*. Dec 17, 2018. Retrieved from https://thehill.com/blogs/blog-briefing-room/news/421684-homelessness-rates-increase-in-us-for-second-straight-year.

Demby, Gene. "For People of Color, a Housing Market Partially Hidden from View." *NPR*. National Public Radio. Jun 17, 2013. Retrieved from https://www.npr.org/sections/codeswitch/2013/06/17/192730233/for-people-of-color-a-housing-market-partially-hidden-from-view.

Desmond, Matthew. "Americans Want to Believe Jobs Are the Solution to Poverty. They're Not." *The New York Times*. The New York Times Co. Sep 11, 2018. Retrieved from https://www.nytimes.com/2018/09/11/magazine/americans-jobs-poverty-homeless.html.

Goodman, Laurie, McCargo, Alanna, and Jun Zhu. "A Closer Look at the Fifteen-Year Drop in Black Homeownership." *Urban Institute*. Urban Wire. Feb 12, 2018. Retrieved from https://www.urban.org/urban-wire/closer-look-fifteen-year-drop-black-homeownership.

Hughes, Becky. "Working Homeless Population Grows in Cities Across the U.S." *Parade*. AMG/Parade. Feb 7, 2018. Retrieved from https://parade.com/643064/beckyhughes/working-homeless-population-grows-in-cities-across-the-u-s/.

Madrigal, Alexis C. "The Racist Housing Policy That Made Your Neighborhood." *The Atlantic*. The Atlantic Monthly Group. May 22, 2014.

Rogers, Adam. "Big Tech Isn't the Problem with Homelessness. It's All of Us." *Wired*. Condé Nast. Jun 21, 2018. Retrieved from https://www.wired.com/story/big-tech-isnt-the-problem-with-homelessness-its-all-of-us/.

Rowe, Michael and Charles Barber. "The Power of Giving Homeless People a Place to Belong." *CityLab*. Jun 12, 2018.

Notes

1. Hughes, "Working Homeless Population Grows in Cities Across the U.S."
2. Desmond, "Americans Want to Believe Jobs Are the Solution to Poverty. They're Not."
3. Rogers, "Big Tech Isn't the Problem with Homelessness. It's All of Us."
4. Daugherty, "Homelessness Rates Increase for Second Straight Year."

5.   Rowe and Barber, "The Power of Giving Homeless People a Place to Belong."
6.   Demby, "For People of Color, a Housing Market Partially Hidden from View."
7.   Goodman, McCargo, and Zhu, "A Closer Look at the Fifteen-Year Drop in Black Homeownership."
8.   Madrigal, "The Racist Housing Policy That Made Your Neighborhood."

The Homeless Crisis Is Getting Worse in America's Richest Cities

By Noah Buhayar and Esmé E. Deprez
Bloomberg Businessweek, November 20, 2018

It was just after 10 p.m. on an overcast September night in Los Angeles, and L. was tired from a long day of class prep, teaching, and grading papers. So the 57-year-old anthropology professor fed her Chihuahua-dachshund mix a freeze-dried chicken strip, swapped her cigarette trousers for stretchy black yoga pants, and began to unfold a set of white sheets and a beige cotton blanket to make up her bed.

But first she had to recline the passenger seat of her 2015 Nissan Leaf as far as it would go—that being her bed in the parking lot she'd called home for almost three months. *The Late Show* with Stephen Colbert was playing on her iPad as she drifted off for another night. "Like sleeping on an airplane—but not in first class," she said. That was in part by design. "I don't want to get more comfortable. I want to get out of here."

L., who asked to go by her middle initial for fear of losing her job, couldn't afford her apartment earlier this year after failing to cobble together enough teaching assignments at two community colleges. By July she'd exhausted her savings and turned to a local nonprofit called Safe Parking L.A., which outfits a handful of lots around the city with security guards, port-a-potties, Wi-Fi, and solar-powered electrical chargers. Sleeping in her car would allow her to save for a deposit on an apartment. On that night in late September, under basketball hoops owned by an Episcopal church in Koreatown, she was one of 16 people in 12 vehicles. Ten of them were female, two were children, and half were employed.

The headline of the press release announcing the results of the county's latest homeless census strikes a note of progress: "2018 Homeless Count Shows First Decrease in Four Years." In some ways that's true. The figure for people experiencing homelessness dropped 4 percent, a record number got placed in housing, and chronic and veteran homelessness fell by double digits. But troubling figures lurk. The homeless population is still high, at 52,765—up 47 percent from 2012. Those who'd become homeless for the first time jumped 16 percent from last year, to 9,322 people, and the county provided shelter for roughly 5,000 fewer people than in 2011.

All this in a year when the economy in L.A., as in the rest of California and the U.S., is booming. That's part of the problem. Federal statistics show homelessness overall has been trending down over the past decade as the U.S. climbed back from the Great Recession, the stock market reached all-time highs, and unemployment sank to a generational low. Yet in many cities, homelessness has spiked.

It's most stark and visible out West, where shortages of shelter beds force people to sleep in their vehicles or on the street. In Seattle, the number of "unsheltered" homeless counted on a single night in January jumped 15 percent this year from 2017—a period when the value of Amazon.com Inc., one of the city's dominant employers, rose 68 percent, to $675 billion. In California, home to Apple, Facebook, and Google, some 134,000 people were homeless during the annual census for the Department of Housing and Urban Development in January last year, a 14 percent jump from 2016. About two-thirds of them were unsheltered, the highest rate in the nation.

At least 10 cities on the West Coast have declared states of emergency in recent years. San Diego and Tacoma, Wash., recently responded by erecting tents fit for disaster relief areas to provide shelter for their homeless. Seattle and Sacramento may be next.

The reason the situation has gotten worse is simple enough to understand, even if it defies easy solution: A toxic combo of slow wage growth and skyrocketing rents has put housing out of reach for a greater number of people. According to Freddie Mac, the government-sponsored housing giant, the portion of rental units affordable to low earners plummeted 62 percent from 2010 to 2016.

Rising housing costs don't predestine people to homelessness. But without the right interventions, the connection can become malignant. Research by Zillow Group Inc. last year found that a 5 percent increase in rents in L.A. translates into about 2,000 more homeless people, among the highest correlations in the U.S. The median rent for a one-bedroom in the city was $2,371 in September, up 43 percent from 2010. Similarly, consultant McKinsey & Co. recently concluded that the runup in housing costs was 96 percent correlated with Seattle's soaring homeless population. Even skeptics have come around to accepting the relationship. "I argued for a long time that the homelessness issue wasn't due to rents," says Joel Singer, chief executive officer of the California Association of Realtors. "I can't argue that anymore."

Homelessness first gained national attention in the 1980s, when declining incomes, cutbacks to social safety net programs, and a shrinking pool of affordable housing began tipping people into crisis. President Ronald Reagan dubiously argued that homelessness was a lifestyle choice. By the mid-2000s, though, the federal government was taking a more productive approach. George W. Bush's administration pushed for a "housing first" model that prioritized getting people permanent shelter before helping them with drug addiction or mental illness. Barack Obama furthered

> **According to Freddie Mac, the government-sponsored housing giant, the portion of rental units affordable to low earners plummeted 62 percent from 2010 to 2016.**

the effort in his first term and, in 2010, vowed to end chronic and veteran homelessness in five years and child and family homelessness by 2020.

Rising housing costs are part of the reason some of those deadlines were missed. The Trump administration's proposal to hike rents on people receiving federal housing vouchers, and require they work, would only make the goals more elusive. Demand for rental assistance has long outstripped supply, leading to years' long waits for people who want help. But even folks who are lucky enough to have vouchers are increasingly struggling to use them in hot housing markets. A survey by the Urban Institute this year found that more than three-quarters of L.A. landlords rejected tenants receiving rental assistance.

It's not bad everywhere. Houston, the fourth-most-populous city in the nation, has cut its homeless population in half since 2011, in part by creating more housing for them. That's dampened the effect of rising rents, Zillow found. Meanwhile, the nonprofit Community Solutions has worked with Chicago, Phoenix, and other cities to gather quality, real-time data about their homeless populations so they can better coordinate their interventions and prioritize spending. The approach has effectively ended veterans' homelessness in eight communities, including Riverside County in California.

Efficiency can go only so far. More resources are needed in the places struggling the most with homelessness. McKinsey calculated that to shelter people adequately, Seattle would have to increase its outlay to as much as $410 million a year, double what it spends now. Still, that's less than the $1.1 billion the consultants estimate it costs "as a result of extra policing, lost tourism and business, and the frequent hospitalization of those living on the streets." Study after study, from California to New York, has drawn similar conclusions. "Doing nothing isn't doing nothing," says Sara Rankin, a professor at Seattle University's School of Law and the director of the Homeless Rights Advocacy Project. "Doing nothing costs more money."

Then there's the moral argument for action. "It's outrageous to me that in a country with so much wealth—and certainly enough for everybody—that there are people who lack even the basics for survival," says Maria Foscarinis, founder and executive director of the National Law Center on Homelessness & Poverty. Appeals to humanity were part of the strategy in the 1980s, when she and other activists helped push through the first major federal legislation to fight homelessness. Her organization has led a charge against laws that make it a crime to sleep outside in public places, one of the more insidious ways politicians have addressed the crisis. In July the U.S. Court of Appeals for the Ninth Circuit affirmed the unconstitutionality of such bans in a case that Foscarinis's group—along with Idaho Legal Aid Services and Latham & Watkins—brought against two such ordinances in Boise. "As long as there is no option of sleeping indoors, the government cannot criminalize indigent, homeless people for sleeping outdoors, on public property, on the false premise they had a choice in the matter," the court wrote. The ruling has led cities, including Portland, Ore., and Berkeley, Calif., to change their policies.

In L.A., Mayor Eric Garcetti has fought to add more shelters and supportive housing, and residents have voted to tax themselves to boost funding by more than

$1 billion. But efforts to build are often delayed or blocked by people who don't want homeless or lower-income people nearby. A strong undercurrent of Nimby-ism—motivated by fear of falling property values, ignorance, racism, or concern over crime—can get nasty. Opponents of proposed homeless shelters took to the streets to protest in Koreatown and spewed boos and catcalls at a town hall in the beach community of Venice. In February the *Los Angeles Times* editorial board implored Garcetti to "step up" and warned that his legacy and political future "will rise or fall on how he handles this colossal urban crisis." (Garcetti, who took office in 2013, is considering a presidential bid in 2020.) Garcetti spokesman Alex Comisar says the city expects to have 15 new emergency shelters opened by mid-2019 and is ahead of schedule with a goal to build 100,000 new housing units by 2021. "Homelessness is the great challenge of our time," he says, "and ending it is Mayor Garcetti's top priority."

To placate angry constituents, officials too often settle for temporary solutions, such as sweeps of tent encampments and street cleaning. San Francisco Mayor London Breed recently scored some publicity, carrying a broom out to the "dirtiest" block in the city for a photo op with the *New York Times*. In other places, there's simply a vacuum of leadership coordinating the patchwork of agencies, nonprofits, and religious organizations trying to help. After reporting intensively for a year on homelessness in the Puget Sound region, the Seattle Times put it bluntly: "No one is in charge."

Meanwhile, the businesses responsible for much of the area's economic fortunes, as well as rising housing costs, have been slow to throw their weight behind solutions. Amazon CEO Jeff Bezos recently earmarked a portion of his $2 billion philanthropic pledge for homeless services—only months after his company fought aggressively to beat back a modest tax on large employers in Seattle that would have raised less than $50 million a year for the same.

Blaming people who are trying to get back on their feet is probably the least productive way to solve the crisis. Consider Mindy Woods, a single mother and U.S. Navy veteran who lives in a Seattle suburb. In 2010 she developed autoimmune diseases that made her chronically tired and caused so much pain she struggled to work at the insurance company where she'd been selling disability policies. "I was just a mess," she says. "I had to quit my job." To help pay rent for the apartment where she lived with her son, she babysat, watched neighbors' pets, and led a Camp Fire youth group. Still, she and her son ended up having to leave the apartment because of a serious mold infestation, kicking off an eight-month period when they couch-surfed and spent time in a motel and shelter. It was a challenge just to refrigerate her son's diabetes medicine.

They eventually were accepted into a transitional apartment, where they stayed for 3½ years. But in 2015 her landlord stopped accepting vouchers. Woods had to race to find another apartment owner who'd take her voucher before it lapsed. Application after application got rejected. "The discrimination was alive and well," she says. Another eight months passed. When she finally found an apartment, there wasn't room for her son. They had no choice but separate, and he now lives nearby.

Woods bristles when people blame the homeless for their predicament. "This is not about drugs, this is not about mental illness, this is not about lazy people," she says. "We were doing everything we could to stay in houses."

There were signs on Election Day that voters on the West Coast want to help. In Portland, a measure to raise more than $650 million for affordable housing won easily. In California, $6 billion in bonds to build more low-income and homeless housing got approved. And in San Francisco, voters supported a measure, backed by Salesforce.com Inc. co-CEO Marc Benioff, to raise taxes on employers to pay for homeless services. These are positive steps. But the hard work of making sure the money gets people housed is just beginning.

Print Citations

CMS: Buhayar, Noah, and Esmé E. Deprez. "The Homeless Crisis Is Getting Worse in America's Richest Cities." In *The Reference Shelf: Affordable Housing*, edited by Micah L. Issit, 109-113. Amenia, NY: Grey House Publishing, 2019.

MLA: Buhayar, Noah, and Esmé E. Deprez. "The Homeless Crisis Is Getting Worse in America's Richest Cities." *The Reference Shelf: Affordable Housing*, edited by Micah L. Issit, Grey House Publishing, 2019, pp. 109-113.

APA: Buhayar, N., & E.E. Deprez. (2019). The homeless crisis is getting worse in America's richest cities. In Micah L. Issit (Ed.), *The reference shelf: Affordable housing* (pp. 109-113). Amenia, NY: Grey House Publishing.

Segregation's Legacy

By Joseph P. Williams

U.S. News and World Report, April 20, 2018

It was designed as both an antidote to rampant housing discrimination under Jim Crow and a path for African-Americans from the ghetto to the middle class.

It swept through Congress and landed on President Lyndon B. Johnson's desk just days after the assassination of Dr. Martin Luther King—and as urban neighborhoods, where days of rioting erupted on news of King's murder, still smoldered.

Before signing the Fair Housing Act of 1968 into law, Johnson called it "among the proudest [moments] of my presidency." Because of it, he predicted, "Negro families [will] no longer suffer the humiliation of being turned away because of their race."

Then, reality set in: Uneven enforcement, deep-seated, cultural bias and the bill's own flaws allowed bigoted mortgage bankers and unscrupulous landlords to preserve—and profit from—the status quo.

Now, a half century after the Fair Housing Act became a civil-rights landmark, multiple studies show housing in America is nearly as segregated as it was when LBJ enacted a law designed to eliminate it. Study after study shows African-Americans still lag far behind whites in home ownership, a key asset in building middle-class wealth.

At the same time, the institutional problems the Fair Housing Act was designed to solve—inequality in mortgage lending and homeownership, as well as real-estate agents steering black home buyers to certain neighborhoods and landlords who avoid renting to minorities—haven't gone away. Limited access to housing in stable, middle-class neighborhoods, analysts say, has had a negative impact on everything from the quality of education black children receive to the health and longevity of their parents.

In 2016, for example, "there were 28,181 reported complaints of housing discrimination" nationwide, according to the National Fair Housing Alliance 2017 annual report. "But we know housing discrimination often goes unreported or undetected. It is estimated that there are over 4 million instances of housing discrimination annually in the rental market alone."

"We still have a very, very segregated society, in terms of housing and [by extension] schools," says John R. Logan, a Brown University sociology professor who specializes in housing discrimination. While there's been "pockets" of improvement, mostly in progressive urban areas, "there's also been some backsliding" in enforcement at the federal and local level.

Meanwhile, widening economic inequality has

> **Study after study shows African Americans still lag far behind whites in home ownership, a key asset in building middle-class wealth.**

emerged as a new, troubling factor in housing discrimination. As the gap widens between rich and poor, African-Americans, who typically earn far less than whites and already face discrimination in the housing market, are in danger of being left further behind.

"The mixture of class and race is hard to disentangle," says Nela Richardson, chief economist at Redfin, a national real estate brokerage and housing analysis firm. On top of de facto segregation, she says, "There are very few neighborhoods where there's economic integration—they're either all rich or all poor. We don't often see a plumber living next to a lawyer living next to a janitor."

Despite troubling data and experts sounding the alarm, Richardson, who studies housing patterns, and others say, don't look to Attorney General Jeff Sessions, Housing and Urban Development Secretary Ben Carson or a Republican-majority Congress to use the Fair Housing Act as a tool to reverse inequality.

Late last month, the *New York Times* reported that the GOP-controlled federal government is actively rolling back its mandate to enforce fair-housing laws, not long after reports that Carson, ordered the words "inclusive" and "free from discrimination" erased from HUD's mission statement. Carson told the *Times* that the notion he's backing away from enforcement of the Fair Housing Act is "absurd," but others aren't convinced.

"Carson has moved at lightning speed to gut these important regulations," says Kristen Clarke, executive director of Lawyers' Committee for Civil Rights Under Law. At the same time, she adds, there's been a marked decline in the number of Justice Department cases brought against realtors or landlords under the Fair Housing Act.

"In both agencies, we've seen significant shifts" away from enforcing the law, Clarke says.

Even former Vice President Walter Mondale, who co-sponsored the bill when it was drafted in 1968, says the progress towards fair and equitable housing has been halting at best.

"There's been a struggle to get the Fair Housing Act recognized as real law, and enforce it at the state and local level," Mondale, who was a senator representing Minnesota when he co-sponsored the bill, told *Time* magazine recently. "I would say we haven't done very well at it. I think it has made significant progress possible in America, but we're not there yet."

That's likely because, besides being a legacy of slavery and Jim Crow laws, discrimination and segregation in housing was at one time sponsored by the federal government itself.

Grappling with the Great Depression in the early 1930s, President Franklin D. Roosevelt implemented a New Deal program to address a housing shortage by building new homes in the suburbs. But the housing programs were "whites only," and the strategy was an official mandate, according to author Richard Rothstein, whose book, *The Color of Law*, examines the government's role in housing discrimination.

In a 2017 interview on *NPR*, Rothstein said the government believed that "if African-Americans bought homes in these suburbs, or even if they bought homes near these suburbs, the property values of the homes they were insuring, the white homes they were insuring, would decline." No evidence supported that assumption, he added.

In fact, when African-Americans tried to buy homes in predominantly white neighborhoods, "property values rose because African-Americans were more willing to pay more [than whites]… simply because their housing supply was so restricted and they had so many fewer choices," Rothstein said.

That meant African-Americans were consigned to live in decaying urban neighborhoods, their children forced to attend underfunded, crumbling schools and get locked out of well-paying jobs. Richardson, the Redfin analyst, says "there are actual physical barriers" between suburban whites, urban neighborhoods "and where the job centers are."

"You'll see a railroad track, a highway, a river—something that literally cuts the [black] community off," she says. "In Cincinnati, the city put a highway that literally cut off this neighborhood in the center of town. And now they're talking about putting a [transit] stop to create another barrier."

Mondale co-sponsored fair-housing legislation with Sen. Edward Brooke, a Massachusetts Republican and the first African-American lawmaker sent to Washington after winning a statewide election. But there was trouble with the bill from the start—particularly enforcement, Mondale said.

In its first years, organizations that were building housing that discriminated—where all whites [lived] and no blacks—would say to the judge, 'Well, this law requires finding a realtor intended to discriminate,'" the former vice president told *Time*. "So there was the difficult, almost impossible task of trying to prove what was in a developer's mind."

Then there was lockstep opposition from Southern Dixiecrats, says Logan, the Brown University sociologist. Even though Johnson himself put his weight behind the law, "racial discrimination and racial segregation wasn't a small thing to them. It was a way of life."

Yet providing equal housing opportunity to black homebuyers and renters is more important than fairness or doing the right thing, Logan says: It's about access to good-paying jobs, government resources, hospitals, parks and even the quality of political representation.

"Segregation and integration was not just about people—it wasn't just housing. It's not about blacks and whites living next to each other," he says. "It was voting, schools, every aspect of life. It was, in a sense, about integrating opportunity. It's also always about resources."

Logan and others say that, overall, things have changed for the better—it's commonplace to see blacks and whites living next to one another, mostly in urban neighborhoods—but some old problems still linger. African-Americans are far more likely than whites to receive high-interest mortgages from banks, real estate agents still "steer" minority buyers away from white communities, and some neighborhood associations still include race-based restrictions on who can move in.

"As a result, in today's America, approximately half of all Black persons and 40 percent of all Latinos live in neighborhoods without a White presence," according to the National Fair Housing Alliance report. "The average White person lives in a neighborhood that is nearly 80 percent White."

It doesn't have to be that way, says Clarke of the Lawyers' Committee for Civil Rights.

"In a perfect world, we have leadership at the federal level" that encourages banks, landlords and investors "to do the right thing," she says. However, "We're not seeing that now, and as a result, we're seeing the resurgence of discrimination in housing markets across the country."

Print Citations

CMS: Williams, Joseph P. "Segregation's Legacy." In *The Reference Shelf: Affordable Housing*, edited by Micah L. Issit, 114-117. Amenia, NY: Grey House Publishing, 2019.

MLA: Williams, Joseph P. "Segregation's Legacy." *The Reference Shelf: Affordable Housing*, edited by Micah L. Issit, Grey House Publishing, 2019, pp. 114-117.

APA: Williams, J.P. (2019). Segregation's legacy. In Micah L. Issit (Ed.), *The reference shelf: Affordable housing* (pp. 114-117). Amenia, NY: Grey House Publishing.

The One Area Where Racial Disparities in Housing Have Disappeared

By Tracy Jan
The Washington Post, May 5, 2017

Racial disparities in subsidized housing—which once saw poor black families over-whelmingly housed in large public developments—have essentially disappeared after decades of inequality, according to a new study by Johns Hopkins University researchers.

But low-income black families are still far more likely than poor whites to live in segregated, impoverished neighborhoods.

The findings show the critical importance of enforcing fair housing laws, researchers said, given the long history of housing discrimination against African Americans. More than half of all children living in subsidized housing in 2011 were black.

Dozens of successful lawsuits have been brought against the U.S. Department of Housing and Urban Development for segregating black families in poor and pre-dominantly minority neighborhoods—which put them at a lifelong disadvantage in education and employment.

Trump officials have indicated they may roll back Obama-era rules instituted to address these disparities. Housing Secretary Ben Carson recently warned against making public housing too comfortable for the poor. Trump has also proposed cutting HUD's budget by 13 percent.

"Black families have been disproportionately represented in inner- city public housing, and there was not an equal opportunity for them to be in multifamily or voucher housing," said Sandra Newman, a Johns Hopkins policy studies professor who lead the research.

In the 1970s, more than 60 percent of black families with subsidized housing lived in public developments, Newman and her co-author found.

The situation was almost the reverse for white families. Only a third of white families with subsidized housing lived in those giant developments, whereas nearly 70 percent chose multifamily units. The privately owned and managed multifamily housing were often in much better physical condition than public developments. Just under 40 percent of black families had access to such housing.

The inequalities persisted through the 1990s. Now, however, the most recent data shows that—largely through the rising use of vouchers—low-income black and white families today have a nearly equal shot at living in privately owned and federally subsidized multifamily units or homes in the private housing market, the study found.

Sixty percent of black families as well as white families with subsidized housing in the 2000s used housing vouchers. A quarter of black families and a fifth of whites lived in public housing projects. And less than a fifth of each race lived in multifamily housing.

"Inequality in access to different kinds of housing has now been completely mitigated," said Newman, who directs the Center on Housing, Neighborhoods and Communities at the university's Institute for Health and Social Policy.

What Accounts for This Shift?

Newman and her co-author, Scott Holupka, cannot determine for sure but said the nature of publicly subsidized housing has changed over the years, with high-rise housing projects being replaced with low-rise townhouses that may be run privately. There's also been a larger movement toward voucher programs that allow families to choose where they want to live.

Newman and Holupka also found no racial differences in the physical quality of public housing projects or how these developments were managed.

There is one area, though, where blacks are faring much worse than whites. Despite having an equal chance at the various types of subsidized housing, African American families are nine times more likely to live in segregated neighborhoods with high poverty and lower home values.

About a third of black households with children who moved into subsidized housing in the 2000s lived in such disadvantaged areas, compared with only 4 percent of whites.

Researchers said this pattern, which held no matter what kind of subsidized housing families chose, could result from various reasons. Housing projects and low-rent units have historically been located in central cities, where there's a disproportionate number of poor African Americans. Black families with children who live in public housing are more than twice as likely as whites to reside in central cities. Landlords in the surrounding suburbs may also discriminate and not rent to black families with vouchers.

> Low-income black families are still far more likely than poor whites to live in segregated, impoverished neighborhoods.

President Obama, toward the end of his term, proposed several initiatives to help poor families move to better neighborhoods, including expanding the voucher program to cover more expensive rent and encourage more landlords to participate.

HUD also strengthened the requirement that communities receiving federal housing funds adhere to the 1968 Fair Housing Act, which prohibits housing discrimination. The new rules require communities to seek out pockets of segregation and poverty; study how low-quality schools, limited jobs and high crime came to be; and put forth remedies.

Newman called the measures "possibly the boldest policy step in recent years" in her paper, published this week in *Housing Policy Debate*.

"It's an attempt to be proactive about assisting tenants to find these higher quality neighborhoods," Newman said. "But HUD is simply ignoring this at the present time."

Critics, including many Republican politicians such as Carson, have objected to such measures as too onerous and have sought to eliminate the new rules.

Print Citations

CMS: Jan, Tracy. "The One Area Where Racial Disparities in Housing Have Disappeared." In *The Reference Shelf: Affordable Housing,* edited by Micah L. Issit, 118-120. Amenia, NY: Grey House Publishing, 2019.

MLA: Jan, Tracy. "The One Area Where Racial Disparities in Housing Have Disappeared." *The Reference Shelf: Affordable Housing,* edited by Micah L. Issit, Grey House Publishing, 2019, pp. 118-120.

APA: Jan, T. (2019). The one area where racial disparities in housing have disappeared. In Micah L. Issit (Ed.), *The reference shelf: Affordable housing* (pp. 118-120). Amenia, NY: Grey House Publishing.

High Housing Costs and Long Commutes Drive More Workers to Sleep in Cars

By Patrick Sisson
Curbed, March 6, 2018

Santa Barbara, California, a coastal enclave boasting beautiful beachfront Spanish missions and a nearly $2 billion tourism industry, offers a postcard view of the state's many natural advantages.

At night, in about a dozen area parking lots attached to churches, nonprofits, and city property, it also provides a look at California's continuing affordability crisis. Known as the Safe Parking Program, the initiative, run by a local nonprofit called the New Beginnings Counseling Center, provides a place to park and rest overnight, as well as connections to local government and charitable resources. These lots form a network of temporary rest spots for low-income workers living out of cars and recreational vehicles with few other options.

According to Safe Parking Program coordinator Cassie Roach, there truly are few options. The city of nearly 92,000 has a 7- to 10-year waitlist for subsidized housing, a single room is hard to find for under $1,000, and the rental market has a 0.6 percent vacancy rate, according to the city (apartment owners argue that's inaccurate). Many of her roughly 150 nightly clients, who spend their evenings in RVs or attempting to doze off in their cars, usually spend their days working: 35 to 40 percent are employed, working as painters, gardeners, servers, and even nurses and veterinarians.

"A lot of the time people have been here in Santa Barbara the majority of the lives," she says. "They have family and friends, and they're established. To go somewhere without family or friends is hard. And living in a vehicle while trying to find a new job is very difficult."

Roach and her team have been trying to solve a unique facet of the affordable housing crisis in the United States. What happens when the working class, tied to jobs and relationships in an area without affordable housing, get pushed past the point of a reasonable commute? For some, cars and RVs end up being the solution.

Behind the Wheel, and Behind on Rent

Housing costs, and homelessness, remain serious concerns across much of the United States, with no easy solutions in sight. According to research from the advocacy group Home1, 11 million Americans spend more than half their paycheck on rent, and the National Low Income Housing Coalition found that a renter making minimum wage working 40 hours a week can reasonably afford a one-bedroom apartment in just 12 counties nationwide. Harvard's Joint Center for Housing Studies found that rent keeps taking a disproportionate chunk of renter income. In 2016, the median renter in the bottom income quartile had just $488 left each month after housing costs, a full 18 percent less, adjusted for inflation, than they did in 2001. Between 2001 and 2011, the JCHS also found that median rental housing costs rose 5 percent, while median renter income dropped 15 percent.

This squeeze—increasing housing costs and stagnating wages—has created a scenario where some people working full-time jobs are living in homeless shelters, or in some cases, camping out in parking lots and along highways. There are no official statistics on the number of working poor using cars and RVs as a home of last resort, but a recent spate of stories on municipalities tackling this issue suggest it's becoming more prevalent, or at least more visible.

Santa Barbara, like much of the country, is seeing its low-income workers increasingly spend more of their lives shuttling to and from work. According to U.S. Census data from 2015, 11,950 of the city's workers, roughly a quarter of the total, commuted more than 50 miles to their job. Nearly a third of those making longer commuters, 2,724 people, make less than $1,250 per month. That's a significant increase from 2002, when only 7,515 made such a long daily trip to work.

Driven in part by the search for affordable housing, rising commute times are an issue both regionally and nationwide, adding even more expenses to full-time workers. Brookings Institution research found that between 2000 and 2012, more Americans took on outsized commutes: The number of jobs within the

> **More time behind the wheel or on a bus or train is taking more money from the working poor.**

typical commute distance for residents in a major metro area fell by 7 percent nationwide. The 2015 American Community Survey found that the country's average commute rose to 26.4 minutes in 2015, and the number of Americans who live in one county and work in another soared from 23.5 million to 40.1 million between 1990 and 2014, a 7 percent increase. More time behind the wheel or on a bus or train is taking more money from the working poor: Data from the Metropolitan Policy Program for the Brookings Institution shows the cost of commuting takes up roughly 6 percent of their income, double that of high-income workers.

In California, especially high-rent coastal areas and the booming Bay Area, many lower-income residents have moved inland to escape ballooning housing costs, leading to a spike in supercommuters. A Pew study found the number of Californians traveling 90 minutes or more to get to work jumped 40 percent between 2005 and 2015. A *New York Times* article in August offered a poignant case study of this phenomenon: an office worker making $81,000 a year who still needs to wake up at 2:15 a.m. for her marathon commute.

The Long Trips of Tourism and Hospitality Workers

Many of these poorly paid supercommuters find themselves working in the hospitality and tourism industries. A recent *Miami Herald* profile detailed the exhausting 13.5-mile round trip of a Hotel Fontainebleau housekeeper that, due to erratic bus schedules, can take between one to three hours each way. Most of her coworkers had a similar story, with commutes lasting two hours or more, four times the county average.

There's a sad calculus to this brutal commute; the article noted they'd have to spent their entire paycheck to afford rent in Miami Beach, where the Fontainebleau is located. As the piece underscores, "a bitter cocktail of exorbitant rents and stagnant wages have pushed workers farther and farther away from the workplace."

A recent survey of workers at Disneyland, based on work by a team of researchers including Occidental College professor Peter Dreier, made headlines for revealing the company's low wages. But as Dreier explained to *Curbed*, Disney also had a disproportionate amount of workers embarking on above-average commutes. Fourteen percent of the park's workers drive more than an hour and a half each way.

"You would think Disney would be aware of how many workers drive more than an hour to make $13 or $14 an hour," he says. "It's so overwhelmingly bigger than the average in Orange County and Los Angeles. Disney should be a leader in this, yet they make the problem worse."

As Dreier notes, Disney has previously campaigned against proposals to bring more workforce housing to Anaheim, which would ostensibly provide more room for their workers. Dreier's research found that, due to juggling family and child care issues with oversized commutes, many workers miss shifts. The company has a serious absenteeism issue; why not use its influence and resources to make things easier for its workforce of more than 30,000?

"People love to be a part of the magic," Drier says. "They love their work, put on a smile, and then they go to sleep in a car, or drive an hour to someplace where they pay 60 percent of their wages for rent."

The physical and financial gap between affordable housing and working-class jobs continues to put stress on workers, even in areas considered hotbeds of economic growth. In Palo Alto, California, the heart of Silicon Valley, city officials have implemented a 72-hour rule for parked vehicles, after the number of RVs parked along area roads has spiked to more than 200 in neighboring communities. Advocates say they're not new arrivals as much as they're residents with fewer and fewer places to go.

"There's this myth that we attract people from all over the place, and it really is a myth," Brian Greenberg of LifeMoves, an organization that helps the homeless, told the *Guardian*. "Most of the people are what I'd say are our people—they graduated from local high schools on the peninsula, in Silicon Valley. People aren't as mobile as one would think."

In Seattle, home to Amazon, where more than 2,300 residents live in their cars, the issue has become serious. A judge recently ruled that if you're living in your car, it can be considered a home based on a interpretation of the Homestead Act, which may significantly change how the city deals with those living in vans and RVs.

While workers choosing to live in vehicles may, in some respects, be the edge cases that draw attention to a wider problem, proximity to work is a serious issue. It's not just about the inconvenience of long commutes. The Brookings Institution's research found that the "suburbanization of poverty" that started in 2000 has meant that both jobs and low-income populations have been shifting geographically. With research showing that, for poor residents, living closer to jobs increases the likelihood of working and leaving welfare, it becomes even more important to link transportation and affordable housing investments with job programs.

With few metro areas managing to match affordable housing construction with job and population growth, many see programs like Santa Barbara's Safe Parking initiative becoming more prevalent. According to Roach, their program is the largest by far, though there are smaller operations in other California cities such as Santa Cruz, San Diego, and San Luis Obispo. And they're received inquiries from Los Angeles, as well as officials in Tennessee and even Pennsylvania, about setting up similar programs. Ever since Roach started in 2015, she has just seen the problem, and the need, get worse.

"The is the worst housing crisis I've ever seen," she says, "and it looks like it's getting more difficult every day."

Print Citations

CMS: Sisson, Patrick. "High Housing Costs and Long Commutes Drive More Workers to Sleep in Cars." In *The Reference Shelf: Affordable Housing,* edited by Micah L. Issit, 121-124. Amenia, NY: Grey House Publishing, 2019.

MLA: Sisson, Patrick. "High Housing Costs and Long Commutes Drive More Workers to Sleep in Cars." *The Reference Shelf: Affordable Housing,* edited by Micah L. Issit, Grey House Publishing, 2019, pp. 121-124.

APA: Sisson, P. (2019). High housing costs and long commutes drive more workers to sleep in cars. In Micah L. Issit (Ed.), *The reference shelf: Affordable housing* (pp. 121-124). Amenia, NY: Grey House Publishing.

Her Six-Hour Commute Each Day Seems Crazy, but Her Affordable Rent Is Not

By Steve Lopez
Los Angeles Times, December 16, 2017

She doesn't need an alarm clock, Carolyn Cherry says. Her brain is programmed, by years of routine, to sound an internal alarm just before 3 a.m.

One hour after rising, she leaves her house in Hemet and drives in darkness to the South Perris Metrolink station, the first leg of her daily journey to work. The drive takes 22 or 23 minutes, a bit longer if she picks up a friend or stops to get a cup of tea for the long train ride ahead. The parking lot is all hers when Cherry arrives, and she pulls into the same spot every time.

The train leaves at 4:43 a.m. and Cherry, 60 years old and a couple of years away from retirement, rides it all the way to the final stop, more than two hours away. That's Union Station in downtown Los Angeles. Scheduled arrival time: 7:05.

Cherry then hustles to the Red Line, pops out of the ground at the Civic Center station, crosses Hill Street and reports for duty as a clerical worker at the L.A. County auditor controller's office by 7:30.

9 Hours of Work, 6 Hours of Commuting a Day

"It's usually 8:15 or 8:20 when I get home at night," says Cherry, who has been doing this merciless long-distance commute for 16 years, getting by on just 4½ hours of sleep each night. "Nine hours of work and six hours of commuting. That's my story."

In a region of hellish commutes, it's one of the craziest I've heard of. But in Southern California, where being close to work is a luxury many in the middle and working class can no longer afford, readers keep telling me to quit pushing affordable housing measures and let the market determine who lives where.

If you can't afford the Westside, they say, go east.

So I went all the way to the end of the line to have a look. And sure, 90 miles or so from downtown L.A., you can get far more stucco for your money. But it comes at a real price.

Ungodly commutes, as we know, are not new to Southern California, which practically invented sprawl. People have long moved out of the city by choice, but with housing costs at historic highs, some now move by necessity.

According to Metro-link, the 400-plus-mile commuter railroad has the longest average one-way trip—36 miles—in the country. Almost two-thirds of Metrolink commuters work in a different county than the one they live in,

> **People have long moved out of the city by choice, but with housing costs at historic highs, some now move by necessity.**

and riders took roughly 600,000 one-way trips of 60 miles or more last year. That sounds grueling, but on a train, at least, you can make good use of your time and experience the evil pleasure of glancing out the window at all the poor souls stuck in traffic.

When Cherry and I board in South Perris, about a dozen other yawners climb aboard, two hours shy of sunrise.

Morning Commute Begins in the Darkness

"This is where I sit," Cherry says as she slides into a four-seat compartment with a table, where she sets her tea.

The Metrolink extension to Perris didn't begin service until the summer of 2016, so before then, Cherry drove to Riverside and took the train the rest of the way. That still added up to three hours each way, and Cherry says she prefers a longer train ride to driving in heavy traffic and contributing to air pollution.

But why Hemet?

Cherry's story unfolds as the train chugs along, with stops in Moreno Valley, Riverside, Corona and Fullerton, the sky outside still dark as empty seats begin to fill.

Terence Dyck says he's in his first week of commuting to a new job in Los Angeles from Nuevo, where he lives in a motor home. It's a long haul, he says, but if the job works out, he'll keep up the commute for a year or so and save money to live closer to work in the future. If he can afford to.

Michael Perkins, a microbiologist heading to the Norwalk station, says he and his wife bought a 3,000-square-foot house in Riverside 10 years ago, with good schools for their three kids. It cost just $280,000. "There's no way I could afford a house like that in L.A.," he says, so for him, an 80-minute door-to-door commute is worth the trouble.

Cherry, a divorced mother of two, lived at the Compton home of her parents in the 1990s and had a neat arrangement with her identical twin sister, Marilyn, who lived in Lynwood. Together, they cared for their aging parents, now deceased, and Marilyn watched Cherry's kids while Cherry was at work.

Lower Housing Costs, but at a Price

Marilyn and her husband, a truck driver, moved to Hemet in 2001 to take advantage of lower housing costs. At the time, Cherry was worried about crime and the quality of schools in Compton, so she decided to head east, too. She rented space in her sister's home in Hemet, kept the child-care arrangement intact, and took on the monster commute to work. In 2009, she and her kids moved into their own home in Hemet.

"It's two bedrooms, two bathrooms, a backyard and amenities I wouldn't be able to afford in Los Angeles on my salary," says Cherry, who makes less than $50,000 a year as a tax services specialist after 25 years on the job.

Her rent is just $800 a month. In L.A., a home like hers would be twice, three times or four times as much. And while Cherry says she has no regrets about her move to Hemet, she does bear some pain. She missed a lot of time with her kids and was not there for some of their social and school activities.

"I was heartbroken a lot of times, and on weekends I made sure I was at their activities," she says. "I felt guilty. A lot of guilt. But I was adamant about my kids having a better life than me."

Her daughter, now 28, graduated from UC San Diego and is a property appraiser for Riverside County. Her son, 23, also went to college and works at Amazon in Riverside.

Cherry looked into making a switch to Riverside or San Bernardino counties, but says the pay was significantly lower, even taking her $400 monthly commuting costs into account. So she decided to hold on to her seniority and retirement benefits, tough out the commute, and retire at 62. Because she works nine-hour days, from 7:30 to 5, she gets every other Monday off, which helps.

No Financial Stress, but Commuter Stress...

"I have no financial stress, whereas if I was in L.A. I'd live paycheck to paycheck. I didn't want to live like that and I didn't want my kids to see us living like that," Cherry says.

"I'm pretty much OK with everything," she continues as her eyes fill and she dabs a tear. "Everything was about sacrifice, and at times I beat myself down because I wasn't educated and didn't have higher pay. But you know what? I did OK, and I helped put my kids through college."

The light is coming up now, and in the distance, L.A. skyscrapers reflect the golden dawn. It's not so bad, says Cherry, once you program yourself to the routine and look forward to seeing the members of your commuting family, including a best friend from junior high who usually boards in Riverside.

"I chat, I sleep, I listen to music, my mind wanders, I think about the past and the future," Cherry says as the train from the land of affordable living arrives on time, halfway through another day of compromise.

Print Citations

CMS: Lopez, Steve. "Her Six-Hour Commute Each Day Seems Crazy, but Her Affordable Rent Is Not." In *The Reference Shelf: Affordable Housing,* edited by Micah L. Issit, 125-128. Amenia, NY: Grey House Publishing, 2019.

MLA: Lopez, Steve. "Her Six-Hour Commute Each Day Seems Crazy, but Her Affordable Rent Is Not." *The Reference Shelf: Affordable Housing,* edited by Micah L. Issit, Grey House Publishing, 2019, pp. 125-128.

APA: Lopez, S. (2019). Her six-hour commute each day seems crazy, but her affordable rent is not. In Micah L. Issit (Ed.), *The reference shelf: Affordable housing* (pp. 125-128). Amenia, NY: Grey House Publishing.

5
Possible Solutions

A number of tiny house villages to house the homeless on a temporary basis, including some for veterans, have been built in several parts of the country. Though residents are glad to have shelter, privacy, and a lock on their doors, critics worry that these communities, already skirting some housing regulations, will turn into permanent substandard housing and are not environmentally sustainable.

Solving the Problem

While there is widespread agreement regarding many of the causes impacting the affordable housing market, there is less agreement regarding the potential solutions. While some strongly advocate for federal housing solutions, others have turned their attention to the private sector and some advocate for solutions blending public and private investment.

The Private and the Public

Affordable housing has long been a government issue with both states and the federal government involvement. The Center for American Progress released a report in 2018 arguing that part of the problem is a basic housing shortage, while former affordable home projects have become increasingly expensive. The CAP therefore proposes that the federal government should reenter the affordable housing system with serious investment. Their report, *Homes for All: A Program Providing Rental Supply Where Working Families Need It Most,* calls for federal investment of $20 billion, which would pay for the construction of 1 million units over the span of the next five years.

According to CAP analyst Michela Zonta, the past record of the Trump administration with regard to this issue makes it unlikely that President Trump or his administration will support a significant federal program to address housing. However, Zonta and CAP hope to help legislators understand the kind of investment that will be needed to solve the housing problem in the future. Further, the *Homes for All* report is intended to help legislators understand the fundamental role that housing plays in the American economy. Since 2010, the number of renter households has increased by 1 million per year, a lasting effect of the Great Recession. Middle- and high-income rental families now occupy units that were once offered at affordable housing rates, increasing competition for remaining affordable property in productive areas. Further, nearly 8 million renting households live on low incomes, but only 4 million units in the United States are offered at affordable rates for persons in that income bracket. The 1 million homes that CAP calls for in the report is considered a starting point for addressing the issue, which might influence market rates and drive costs downward for other units. Affordable units could then reduce government subsidies currently being given to families to house them in more expensive units, and the government could then shift subsidies to other low-income individuals and families.[1]

For Zonta and CAP, the housing crisis is a supply issue and can be addressed by increasing the supply of affordable housing. Others disagree and argue that government intervention in the housing market is, and perhaps has always been, bad for consumers. Writing in an essay published by the pro-free market *Hoover Institution*,

Richard A. Epstein argues that the primary problem with the housing market is government regulation. Specifically, Epstein argues that bureaucracies of local officials have claimed discretionary authority over the housing market through a variety of fees, taxes, and permits that present a burden to developers. The argument is that the removal of burdens and barriers to development will drive down the cost of construction and that developers will choose to develop low-cost units to take advantage of the growing market for such units. While some developers would still target the luxury and high-cost markets, others might concentrate on low-cost development to avoid competition for luxury units, while others might choose to develop properties at various ends of the spectrum. Epstein argues that developers tend to gravitate toward higher-end properties because of burdensome planning, permitting, and construction costs compared to the potential profit of low-income rentals. This situation, Epstein argues, means that costs continue to increase, leading activists to call for reforms and subsidies, which he argues props up the inflated market rather than helping to reduce costs.[2]

One idea that has become increasingly popular among progressives is the idea of imposing a luxury tax on high-end development that could be used to fund affordable development. Writing in 2017, financial journalist Eric Uhlfelder described how such a program was used to fund affordable housing in New York when Battery Park City was in development in Manhattan. At the time, the city proposed that developers needed to include low-income housing within the Battery Park development, but Sandy Frucher, then head of the Battery Park City Authority, discovered through her own research that poor and minority leaders preferred subsidies to help improve housing within their own communities. As a result, part of the profits from the high-end developments in Battery City Park were used to create rent-stabilized apartments in other neighborhoods.[3]

One recent proposal in this vein came from Senator Elizabeth Warren, who has proposed a 2 percent tax on assets of more than $50 million, and 3 percent on assets over $1 billion. University of California, Berkeley, economists Emmanuel Saez and Gabriel Zucman helped to design the wealth tax, which would impact roughly 75,000 families and raise $2.75 trillion over a decade. The idea is to make it less and less advantageous for the ultra-wealthy to "hoard" wealth, while the program would reward charitable giving and spending, but would continually penalize permanent assets over $50 million.[4] Critics of this idea have argued that the wealthy already pay a disproportionate share of the income tax and that this relatively small number of Americans also has more of an impact on the economy and so should not be penalized for their success given that their activities create and fund jobs.[5]

Alternative Solutions

The limited success of government-operated solutions has inspired efforts to find solutions to the housing problem from alternative sources. Recently, this included a $500 million program designed by Microsoft to address housing shortages in Seattle, and a Citigroup privately funded program to create affordable housing using land trusts. Likewise, a number of states have developed a hybrid of public-private investment, such as the popular "inclusive zoning" measures adopted by some cities and states in which private developers are required to leave aside units for affordable housing when engaging in new developments.

In some areas, housing pressures and affordability have created a fad involving "tiny houses," extra small units that can be constructed from kits or on site for a fraction of the cost of standard-sized houses. Tiny houses are essentially like building self-sustained house additions or modest apartments, which can be linked to sewage and utility systems or can utilize alternative measures, like composting toilets, etc. Advocates have argued that tiny houses save space, increase density and efficiency, and provide a road to independence for individuals who cannot afford to enter the mainstream housing market and feel they are wasting income on rental when that same income could buy a more affordable home, like a tiny home.[6] Kevin Polk, executive director of the American Tiny House Association, believes that tiny houses might be able to help solve problems like homelessness, and the US Interagency Council on Homelessness supported the idea in a 2017 report. That year, a tiny house "village" was established near Kansas City, as part of an effort to re-house homeless veterans, called the Veteran Community Project. Similar projects have been started in Seattle, Washington, Nashville, Tennessee, and in upstate New York.[7]

However, critics of the tiny house movement have raised some troubling issues. First, by housing people in small self-contained houses rather than in densely packed apartments, tiny houses are inefficient and contribute to the need for more land, rather than pushing construction and housing vertically, which increases density. By contributing to sprawl, tiny houses also increase CO_2 emissions and so pose a negative contribution to the nation's global warming problem. This is similar to what happens when development spreads to suburbs rather than increasing urban density. Studies have found, for instance, that the average person in San Francisco city emits 6.7 metric tons of CO_2 per year, while each individual in the sprawled Bay Area emits more than double that amount, at 14.6 metric tons.[8] Other critics have pointed out that the tiny house movement has done little to encourage racial diversity, with communities and tiny house organizations being predominantly white.

While some see the criticisms of the tiny house movement as insignificant compared to the potential to provide affordable housing for the homeless or low-income families, the basic concept has significant detriments. Any type of community is only sustainable so long as residents of that community have access to amenities and resources. Most of America's resources are concentrated in its cities and so providing for individuals and families means creating a better flow of resources from the cities and other productive areas to consumers. Building sprawling communities isolated from urban centers, in which individuals each occupy their own building rather than living in collective units, is not an efficient use of resources or land. By adopting this potential solution, communities may be embarking on another unsustainable path that ultimately deepens environmental problems and future housing needs. Writing in Jacobin magazine, Arielle Milkman sees the tiny house issue as part of a much deeper problem in the American imagination and believes that proponents of the movement are perpetuating ideas about individualistic property ownership and the pleasure of conquering new frontiers, when solving America's economic and housing problem actually requires creating dense, friendly cities in which residents sacrifice independence for access to the benefits of citizenship.[9]

Works Used

Anzilotti, E. "This Plan Shows How Government Should Get Back in the Housing Business." *Fast Company*. Jul 24, 2018. Retrieved from https://www.fastcompany.com/90204034/this-plan-shows-how-government-should-get-back-in-the-housing-business.

Epstein, Richard A. "The Affordable Housing Crisis." *Hoover Institution*. Feb 27, 2017. Retrieved from https://www.hoover.org/research/affordable-housing-crisis.

Matthews, Dylan. "The Case against Tiny Houses." *Vox*. Vox Media. Sep 26, 2016. Retrieved from https://www.vox.com/a/new-economy-future.

Milkman, Arielle. "The Tiny House Fantasy." *Jacobin*. Jan 19, 2016. https://www.jacobinmag.com/2016/01/tiny-house-movement-nation-tumbleweed-environment-consumerism/.

Plunkett, Mike. "Tiny Houses Multiply amid Big Issues as Communities Tackle Homelessness." *The Washington Post*. Oct 26, 2018. Retrieved from https://www.washingtonpost.com/graphics/2018/national/tiny-houses/.

Sisson, Patrick. "Tiny Houses: Big Future, or Big Hype?" *Curbed*. Jul 18, 2017. Retrieved from https://www.curbed.com/2017/7/18/15986818/tiny-house-zoning-adu-affordable-housing.

Tanzi, Alexandre. "Top 3% of U.S. Taxpayers Paid Majority of Income Tax in 2016." *Bloomberg*. Oct 14, 2018. Retrieved from https://www.bloomberg.com/news/articles/2019-02-07/trump-says-he-s-open-to-changing-salt-deduction-cap-in-tax-law.

Uhlfelder, Eric. "How Cities Should Take Care of Their Housing Problem." *The New York Times*. The New York Times Co. Feb 21, 2017. Retrieved from https://www.nytimes.com/2017/02/21/opinion/how-cities-should-take-care-of-their-housing-problems.html.

Yglesias, Matthew. "Elizabeth Warren's Proposed Tax on Enormous Fortunes, Explained." *Vox*. Vox Media. Jan 24, 2019. Retrieved from https://www.vox.com/policy-and-politics/2019/1/24/18196275/elizabeth-warren-wealth-tax.

Notes

1. Anzilotti, "This Plan Shows How Government Should Get Back in the Housing Business."
2. Epstein, "The Affordable Housing Crisis."
3. Uhlfelder, "How Cities Should Take Care of Their Housing Problems."
4. Yglesias, "Elizabeth Warren's Proposed Tax on Enormous Fortunes, Explained."
5. Tanzi, "Top 3% of U.S. Taxpayers Paid Majority of Income Tax in 2016."

6. Sisson, "Tiny Houses: Big Future, or Big Hype?"
7. Plunkett, "Tiny Houses Multiply amid Big Issues as Communities Tackle Homelessness."
8. Matthews, "The Case Against Tiny Houses."
9. Milkman, "The Tiny House Fantasy."

Private-Sector Solution to Affordable Housing Gets Off the Ground

By Laura Kusisto

The Wall Street Journal, April 26, 2018

A new initiative will provide funding to nonprofits looking to buy land and build homes for lower- and middle-income families, in an effort to address affordability challenges gripping cities from Pittsburgh to New Orleans.

The venture, funded by Citi Community Development, which is affiliated with Citigroup Inc., and administered by Grounded Solutions Network, a non-profit, will distribute $500,000 to local groups with the aim of turning land trusts into a more significant provider of affordable housing.

The move comes as once-affordable American cities are struggling to provide housing to families with modest incomes.

One solution are nonprofits that acquire city land or buy land and buildings in areas that are still relatively affordable and sell homes to those families, with the stipulation that they resell them for a modest price.

The advantage of the "land trust" model is that the homes built on the land are affordable in perpetuity. Under the most common form of affordable-housing production—housing built using tax credits—developers typically have the right to convert it to market-rate housing after several decades.

But there are few new sources of federal funding for affordable housing, and land trusts have struggled to grow.

Citi Community Development, which focuses on economic development in underserved communities, is giving $1 million in total to the initiative. The "accelerator" funding will be distributed to a number of nonprofits in places that Citigroup serves to help fulfill federal regulatory requirements. The remaining $500,000 will be used to provide technical assistance and online tools to land trusts.

"The idea of getting to scale has been a dream of the community land trust movement for several years. I think we have a chance to do exactly what the name says—to accelerate the growth of land trusts in various markets around the country," said Tony Pickett, chief executive of Grounded Solutions Network, which helps foster land trusts around the U.S. and will help distribute the funds.

There are now 225 land trusts around the U.S., in places ranging from Austin to San Francisco, but many of them remain small. One of the largest is in Burlington, Vt., with about 600 owner-occupied homes on its land.

Groups in New York City last year started a land trust that leaders say could quickly grow to be one of the largest in the country, with 250 homes in the next couple of years. It faces particular challenges given the high cost of land in the city.

Land trusts grew out of the civil-rights movement and were seen as a way to help African Americans acquire property and solidify voting rights, Mr. Pickett said. The first was in Albany, Ga.

Land trusts are still a relatively untested concept in major cities such as New York, and they face significant hurdles. They often must compete against private developers, who are willing to pay a premium for land, especially in the current hot market.

Many policymakers are also wary of promoting homeownership for less wealthy families, given that federal policies that promoted homeownership among such households helped lead to the housing bust. Land trusts carefully screen potential purchasers and typically restrict the price at which owners can re-sell their homes from to prevent speculation and carefully screen potential purchasers.

Land-trust supporters say that helping low- and middle-income families buy homes is an important alternative to affordable rental housing, which offers less long-term stability and gives them little opportunity to build wealth.

> **Home prices have shot up in recent years and continue to rise at about twice the rate of incomes. Mortgage rates are also rising, which makes homeownership even less affordable.**

"Homeownership really has become a proxy for wealth and for race and it's increasingly out of reach," said Bob Annibale, global director of Citi Community Development and Inclusive Finance.

A typical homeowner household saw its net worth grow 15% from 2013 to 2016, while a typical renter or other non-owner household saw its net worth decline by 5% during the same period, according to a report last fall by the Federal Reserve.

Those gains differ sharply by race, 50 years after the creation of the Fair Housing Act, which was intended to reduce racial disparities in homeownership. The overall U.S. homeownership rate rose to 64.2% in the fourth quarter of 2017 from 63.6% a year earlier, according to the U.S. Census Bureau. But the homeownership rate among black families sat at 42.1%.

Home prices have shot up in recent years and continue to rise at about twice the rate of incomes. Mortgage rates are also rising, which makes homeownership even less affordable. In addition, rising rents and student loan debt also have made it challenging for renters to save for a down payment.

"There's also, especially in most of the major high-growth markets a growing concern about gentrification and displacement," Mr. Pickett said. People "are being displaced. They are being pushed further and further from job centers."

Print Citations

CMS: Kusisto, Laura. "Private-Sector Solution to Affordable Housing Gets Off the Ground." In *The Reference Shelf: Affordable Housing,* edited by Micah L. Issit, 137-139. Amenia, NY: Grey House Publishing, 2019.

MLA: Kusisto, Laura. "Private-Sector Solution to Affordable Housing Gets Off the Ground." *The Reference Shelf: Affordable Housing,* edited by Micah L. Issit, Grey House Publishing, 2019, pp. 137-139.

APA: Kusisto, L. (2019). Private-sector solution to affordable housing gets off the ground. In Micah L. Issit (Ed.), *The reference shelf: Affordable housing* (pp. 137-139). Amenia, NY: Grey House Publishing.

Microsoft's $500 Million Plan to Fix Seattle's Housing Problem, Explained

By Dylan Matthews
Vox, January 23, 2019

Microsoft has announced an unusual bit of corporate political activism: $500 million to support affordable housing in the Seattle area, where rents have shot up considerably as tech workers there and at Amazon have moved in.

Specifically, as the *Seattle Times*'s Vernal Coleman and Mike Rosenberg explain, the company is spending $225 million on below-market-rate loans to developers to build affordable housing in suburbs to the east of Seattle (like Redmond, where Microsoft is headquartered), targeting families earning between $62,000 and $124,000; $250 million on market-rate loans for developers to build low-income housing (targeting households earning up to 60 percent of the area median income, so as to limit to poorer families); and another $25 million in grants to local groups addressing homelessness.

In the day or so since the plan was announced, I've seen two kinds of takes. There's the tech booster take: Look, our coding overlords aren't so bad! And there's the cynical anti-capitalist take: This is a rich company trying to pay indulgences when we should just be taxing it to solve these problems.

The cynical anti-capitalist take is absolutely 100 percent right about this much: Microsoft's initiative, with the exception of that last $25 million going to grants, is not philanthropy. 95 percent of the money is going into for-profit loans that will make the company money.

Yes, there's an argument to be made that some of these loans wouldn't be offered absent Microsoft's injection of capital, as it's more profitable to finance high-rent developments if you can only build so many units. Maybe the initiative will reshuffle local developers' portfolios to make them build more low-rent apartment buildings, duplexes, etc. That would be beneficial. But we typically don't categorize profitable activities as philanthropy.

It Won't Fix the Problem, but It's a Good Move Anyway

That said, I think the Microsoft move is probably a net good for the world. As Mike Rosenberg (who's one of the best housing reporters in the country, and whom you should follow in Twitter if you're at all interested in the topic) notes, Microsoft also got the mayors of various nearby Seattle suburbs, including Redmond but also Bellevue, Kirkland, and Kent, to commit to upzoning: relaxing zoning rules to allow developers to build structures with more units.

The mayors promise to "consider opportunities" to "increase density near current and planned public transit," "reduce or waive parking requirements in transit corridors," streamline permitting for low-income housing, and on and on and on.

Of course, what's happening here is, in some ways, more nefarious-sounding than the arch anti-capitalist take presumed: Microsoft is not merely trying to buy support; it's also pressuring local politicians into changing policies to fit its priorities. From a company with as much money, and as many local residents dependent on it for their livelihood, as Microsoft, that kind of pressure is formidable, and kind of disturbing.

But here's the thing: These policy changes are what could actually transform Seattle from a place where new high-paying tech jobs are net-negative for poor residents to one where they're net-positive.

As Matt Yglesias explained in the context of Amazon's HQ2 search, booms helping out high-income workers appear to make things actively worse for poor people in places with tight housing markets, where rents are high due to scarcity.

In places with slack housing markets, where rents aren't being bid up and housing is plentiful, influxes of rich workers appear to make life better for poor residents, who both get new wealthy customers at their jobs *and* can afford their rent.

In the *New York Times*, E. Tammy Kim called for Seattle and cities in a similar situation to impose targeted taxes on companies that employ many high earners. She calls the proposal "akin to a pollution tax," with the new employees joining the city and renting apartments serving as the pollution in this analogy.

> These policy changes are what could actually transform Seattle from a place where new high-paying tech jobs are net-negative for poor residents to one where they're net-positive.

While high tax brackets on rich people certainly have plenty of merit (and Washington currently lacks any income tax at all), this specific plan is a weird second-best to a normal progressive income tax, and would have the unintended consequence of deterring businesses from raising wages for fear of running afoul of the "you have too many high-paid employees" penalty. But more importantly, Kim's whole argument sort of misses the point of having cities. Seattle is expensive because it's a really, really nice place to live. That's a problem because for years, the supply of housing hasn't kept up with demand.

The solution isn't to try to reduce demand by pressuring businesses into going somewhere else, because too many people want to live in this great city. The solution is to make it affordable enough that everyone who wants to live there can live there. That could include subsidies for low-income people, affordable housing requirements, expanded public housing, and the like—but it also has to involve making it legal throughout the city and suburbs to build apartment developments large enough to fit everyone.

The real way to remedy Seattle's problem is to turn the Seattle area into a slack housing market. And these kinds of mayoral pledges suggest that the city's suburbs are getting interested in doing that.

Print Citations

CMS: Matthews, Dylan. "Microsoft's $500 Million Plan to Fix Seattle's Housing Problem, Explained." In *The Reference Shelf: Affordable Housing,* edited by Micah L. Issit, 140-142. Amenia, NY: Grey House Publishing, 2019.

MLA: Matthews, Dylan. "Microsoft's $500 Million Plan to Fix Seattle's Housing Problem, Explained." *The Reference Shelf: Affordable Housing,* edited by Micah L. Issit, Grey House Publishing, 2019, pp. 140-142.

APA: Matthews, D. (2019). Microsoft's $500 million plan to fix Seattle's housing problem, explained. In Micah L. Issit (Ed.), *The reference shelf: Affordable housing* (pp. 140-142). Amenia, NY: Grey House Publishing.

Tiny Houses: Salvation for the Homeless or a Dead End?

By Paul Lewis
The Guardian, March 23, 2017

Othello Village is on a plot of land behind a gas station, surrounded by a chain-link fence. It consists of 28 wooden huts and 12 tents that flap in a bitter Pacific wind. Residents share a shower, toilet and kitchen tent, with food stored in plastic boxes to keep out the rats.

Until recently the cabins lacked heating or electricity, and the children who live there – currently 11 of its 67 inhabitants—had to use flashlights to read their schoolbooks. This is how Seattle, one of the richest cities in the world, flush with cash from Amazon and Microsoft, houses some of its poorest residents.

Seattle is not alone. Wooden cabins euphemistically referred to as tiny houses are increasingly viewed as a quick and cheap solution to homelessness and, with minimal public debate, they are mushrooming across the country.

The shed-like structures have appeared in vacant lots and scrubland in at least 10 states, from Florida to New York to Utah. But the trend is most apparent in northern California and the Pacific north-west. Some of America's most liberal cities have in recent years shifted from banning and clearing unauthorized homeless settlements, based in part on the argument they were unfit for habitation, to sanctioning and even funding camps that skirt building regulations thanks to loopholes or special dispensation.

Depending on who you ask, moving homeless people into tiny houses is either a pragmatic means of rescuing them from the street or an alarming shift in urban planning that could pave the way for the creation of shantytowns.

Barbara Poppe, who coordinated federal homelessness policy for most of Barack Obama's presidency, said she believes the development of slums is a real risk and that some of the ramshackle camps used for homeless people are "completely deplorable."

"Why would we accept that people should be living in huts that don't have access to water, electricity and sanitation?" she said, adding that such basic accommodation stigmatizes homeless people.

Poppe now works as a leading homelessness consultant. She was recently hired by Seattle's mayor, Ed Murray, to review the city's homelessness strategy. She advised against funding tiny house encampments, arguing the money would be better spent constructing permanent affordable housing. The city is going ahead with them regardless.

"I always challenge the folks on the west coast about this," Poppe said. "I say, 'I don't understand why you find it acceptable for children and infants to live like this.'" The response, Poppe added, is often a blank stare and a stock reply: "We have to do something. This is better than doing nothing."

"It's Empowering for the People Involved"

That's also the view of residents of Othello, which opened last year.

They say they are grateful for the lockable doors on their cabins, which offer more privacy than city shelters. Shelters are also often at capacity and exclude many homeless people with rules barring couples and pets.

The rules tend to be more flexible in tiny-house and tent encampments, some of which were born of previously unauthorized camps run by homeless people. Othello is self-managed, with rotations for chores such as manning the security gate.

"It's self-organization, it's empowering for the people involved," said Sean Smith, a former cook who moved into his cabin a couple of months ago. "As opposed to feeling crushed under the weight of circumstance."

Smith, who was born in Seattle and has spent much of the past three decades homeless, conceded the tiny house was rudimentary. "It's a wooden tent, that's what it is, basically," he said. "Sure, I got structure, I got the ability to lock the door. I would love to see a fully functioning village where each unit is actually a home."

He added that someone could "get hypothermia in one of these."

Even so, Smith and others objected last month when the nonprofit that supports the camp raised enough money to connect the huts to electricity, bringing heat and light. They felt the money would be better spent on constructing more tiny houses, because homeless people inquire about vacancies on a daily basis.

The ethics of tiny homes seem more fraught when their youngest inhabitants are taken into account.

On the other side of Seattle, on land owned by the Lutheran Church of the Good Shepherd, there is a cluster of 14 cabins. Their residents include a woman named Rhonda, who became homeless after losing her job as a restaurant manager. She said she was grateful for the shelter but was finding it a cramped place in which to bring up her five-year-old daughter, Brooklyn.

"She's got a lot of energy," she said. "There's just no room. No TV. Nothing to do." Her daughter would often rather sit in a car, she said, than spend hours inside the one-room cabin.

Sharon Lee, executive director of Seattle's Low Income Housing Institute, which manages both settlements, stressed that the cabins are supposed to be temporary accommodation. "We don't want tiny houses to be a dead end," she said.

She hit upon the concept after decades navigating restrictive building codes and planning rules that made it impossible to build cheap and quick housing for homeless people; Lee was thrilled to discover "a bit of a loophole" whereby structures smaller than 120-square feet are not recognized as permanent dwellings. Tiny houses costing a mere $2,200 would be exempt from regulations governing residential buildings.

Seattle—which has declared a state of emergency over its homelessness crisis – threw its support behind the initiative, granting special permission for clusters of cabins on public and private land across the city and giving Lee $1.24m to run various sites in 2017. By the end of the year, her organization will have 127 cabins at five locations, providing shelter to more than 310 men, women and children.

> **Wooden cabins, euphemistically referred to as tiny houses, are mushrooming across the country.**

The city insists they are only a stopgap solution, and the ultimate goal is to move tiny-house residents into permanent homes. Lee said she has achieved this with 161 people.

But she conceded there was a shortage of places where people could move. Seattle's lack of affordable housing has contributed to what Lee calls the worst homelessness crisis of her 25-year career. Her own organization owns or manages around 2,000 units of affordable housing and is constantly building more, but it can take three to four years for any one project to come to fruition. The situation may be helped by a huge property-tax levy for low-income housing that was approved by voters last year.

In the meantime, "you have to put homeless people somewhere," Lee said. "If the shelters can't take them, where should they be? On the streets?"

This is not the only indication that tiny-house villages may be an enduring presence.

Ten encampments of shed-like structures for homeless people are planned for the end of 2017 in San Jose, in an area where the expansion of technology giants such as Google, Apple and Facebook has contributed to an acute housing shortage and soaring rental costs. It is the most ambitious tiny-house experiment in the country.

Ray Bramson, a manager at the city's housing department, said the aim is for every occupant of a tiny house to be moved into permanent housing within five years, a goal bolstered by the recent approval of a local ballot measure that will channel hundreds of millions of dollars into affordable homes. In any event, the California legislation that allows San Jose to bypass building and safety rules for its tiny houses expires in 2022.

Yet Bramson conceded that "things could change" and that if the demand persists, the legislation could be renewed. "If these continue to be viable we would absolutely look into whether they could stay longer," he said.

Andrew Heben, who helped start a tiny-house village in Oregon and has documented their rise in his book, *Tent City Urbanism*, said that virtually all of them began as temporary encampments that cities only reluctantly agreed to. But he said he was unaware of any that have been shut down.

"Most cities insist on the 'temporary' designation even though they know these will be needed into the foreseeable future," he said.

A Growing Movement

The movement is burgeoning. In Los Angeles and Oakland, both cities that have resisted efforts for city-approved communities of tiny houses, activists have been distributing homemade varieties in unsanctioned acts of guerilla philanthropy. An artist named Gregory Kloehn has built some 50 tiny houses and distributed them to homeless people in West Oakland.

But if tiny houses for homeless people are indeed destined to become permanent features of the cityscape, some say they must meet a higher standard. There is added urgency, Heben argues, because the need for them will almost certainly increase under the Trump administration. The Republican president has, for example, proposed cutting billions of dollars from the Department of Housing and Urban Development, which funds affordable housing.

Heben's second village, which he begins construction on this month, will be a permanent community consisting of 250-square feet structures – small as opposed to tiny – with en-suite bathrooms and even kitchenettes.

They will cost $60,000 per unit rather than $3,300, as at Heben's inaugural project, yet they will still only be a third of the price of conventional affordable housing in Eugene.

These sorts of comparatively comfortable tiny homes already exist at Quixote village in Olympia, the state capital of Washington. Some view it as the gold-standard for tiny house communities. Ten of the original 30 residents who moved in three years ago have stayed, and some have signaled they want to remain for good. Quixote "is almost the pinnacle of their aspirations," said Alan, 66, a resident for two years.

Showers and shared kitchen facilities are in a warm, permanent building, rather than the canvas tents used sixty miles away in Seattle. Every tiny house has a porch and a bathroom. As an equal proportion of the development's total price tag, each house costs $88,000; on an individual basis they are $19,000 per unit.

Alan said that he and his ex-wife, both nurses, once had a combined income of $100,000 and a 32ft sailboat. But their divorce tipped him into a downward spiral, and he spent more than a decade living in a homemade shack, on the streets, and in a Salvation Army shelter.

He recalled the feeling when he first moved into his tiny home in Quixote just over two years ago. "The ability to go in the cabin, close the door, lie on the bed – utter relief," he said. "Like reaching the shore after a shipwreck."

Alan reads for as many as 18 hours a day – "it is probably the most extreme, intense, escapism," he said – and there are *New Yorker* covers decorating the walls of his cabin and books stacked in every corner. On the windowsill is a book that documents how shantytowns appeared across Seattle during the Great Depression.

Might tiny houses for homeless people also be described as shanties?

"That's a viewpoint taken from high above," he said. "To the people out there on streets, living in cardboard boxes in alleyways, this represents the promised land."

Print Citations

CMS: Lewis, Paul. "Tiny Houses: Salvation for the Homeless or a Dead End? In *The Reference Shelf: Affordable Housing,* edited by Micah L. Issit, 143-147. Amenia, NY: Grey House Publishing, 2019.

MLA: Lewis, Paul. "Tiny Houses: Salvation for the Homeless or a Dead End? *The Reference Shelf: Affordable Housing,* edited by Micah L. Issit, Grey House Publishing, 2019, pp. 143-147.

APA: Lewis, P. (2019). Tiny houses: Salvation for the homeless or a dead end? In Micah L. Issit (Ed.), *The reference shelf: Affordable housing* (pp. 143-147). Amenia, NY: Grey House Publishing.

Nine Rules for Better Housing Policy

By Jenny Schuetz

The Brookings Institution, May 2, 2018

Earlier this year, HUD Secretary Ben Carson raised eyebrows when he proposed changing the agency's mission statement, removing references to "sustainable, inclusive communities." Changes to HUD's mission statement reflect an underlying problem. The U.S. does not have, nor has it ever had, a comprehensive vision for housing policy. Rather, many separate policies enacted by federal, state, and local government agencies affect housing markets. Only 4 percent of U.S. households (about 5 million low-income families) receive housing subsidies from the federal government. But the availability, quality, cost, and location of housing matters to all Americans.

In this article, I examine six goals that housing policy should try to achieve—and three pitfalls it should avoid. Future articles will describe current policies that impact housing outcomes and how they should be adapted to better achieve social and economic goals.

Goal 1: Housing should not harm the health and safety of families or communities.

In the late 19th century, progressive reformers worried about how tenement buildings endangered poor families. The lack of fresh air and running water, combined with overcrowding, encouraged the spread of contagious diseases. Policies such as minimum quality building standards are necessary to protect families and communities. Unlike in earlier eras, today's housing quality deficiencies may not be readily observable by prospective residents. Examples include lead-based paint or asbestos, which can be particularly dangerous for children. Residents of Flint, Mich. and other localities unknowingly drank unsafe water from public utilities for years. Poorly designed or maintained buildings may also harm neighbors. For instance, fires in unsafe buildings cause devastating human and financial damage to communities.

Goal 2: Information about housing transactions should be clear, so that people and companies can make good decisions.

Many housing market activities—searching for a rental apartment, signing a lease, taking out a mortgage—are complicated legal and financial transactions. Often one

party involved has more information than others. For instance, during the mid-2000s
housing boom, many borrowers signed mortgage contracts
they did not fully understand

> **The U.S. does not have, nor has it ever had, a comprehensive vision for housing policy.**

and could not repay. To make sure that parties do not enter into agreements that
they don't understand or that don't reflect their true willingness to pay, public policy
should require appropriate information disclosures and provide redress for deliberately withholding relevant information.

Goal 3: Housing location, construction, and maintenance should improve environmental sustainability and resilience.

To mitigate environmental impacts, public policy should encourage thoughtful
placement of new housing and increased use of clean building materials and tech-
nologies. Houses are one of the primary sources of energy consumption, requiring
fuel and other natural resources for construction, heating and cooling, and daily
activities. Transportation systems that move families between their homes and jobs
consume large amounts of energy and create greenhouse gas emissions. Housing
location patterns—especially proximity to water—also affect communities' vulner-
ability to the impacts of climate change.

Goal 4: Housing supply should be able to expand to meet demand.

State, regional, and national policymakers should reduce barriers to housing supply
erected by local governments. Housing supply is critical to economic growth. In regions where housing is scarce or too expensive, firms will have difficulty hiring and
retaining workers and young people will delay forming new households. In aggregate, the nation's productivity will suffer. Local governments in some of the country's most productive regions, particularly the West Coast and the Northeast, have
adopted overly restrictive land use regulation that constrains housing growth and
drives up prices. These policies are popular with current homeowners, but they reduce state and national economic well-being. Moreover, they systematically exclude
young workers and lower-income families from living near employment centers and
in communities that provide economic opportunity.

Goal 5: All families should have access to neighborhoods that offer economic opportunity.

Policymakers should reduce barriers to high-opportunity neighborhoods, both by
prohibiting discrimination today and addressing longstanding wealth gaps caused
by past discrimination. Where families live have important implications for their
economic, physical, social, and emotional well-being. Location is particularly critical for children: The neighborhood in which they live determines what schools they
attend and which children become their friends. For most of U.S. history, housing

discrimination has restricted African-Americans from living in high-opportunity neighborhoods. Fifty years after the Fair Housing Act banned discrimination based on race, color, religion, sex, or national origin, most metropolitan areas still suffer from high levels of racial and economic segregation.

Goal 6: To help poor families achieve housing stability, increase their incomes.

All families need a safe, stable, healthy place to live. Housing instability and persistent financial stress harms families' economic, physical, and emotional well-being. But the poorest 20 percent of U.S. families have too little income to afford even minimum quality housing. In most parts of the U.S., affordability problems for poor families reflect low wages and insufficient jobs, not excessively high housing costs. The most direct solution is therefore to supplement the incomes of poor families. Unless there are other indicators that local housing markets are not functioning well—for instance, excess regulation is driving up housing costs—supply-side policies are likely to introduce further distortions and will help fewer families for the same amount of money.

Pitfall 1: Don't subsidize housing in some locations more than in others.

Policymakers should consider the impacts of programs that explicitly or implicitly favor certain types of locations. For instance, transportation policies that prioritize cars and highways over mass transit implicitly benefit suburbs and rural areas, with negative environmental impacts. Federal assistance for rebuilding homes damaged by fires or hurricanes subsidize areas prone to natural disasters and encourage future construction in those same vulnerable locations.

Pitfall 2: Don't subsidize homeownership over renting.

U.S. tax policy provides vastly larger subsidies to homeowners than to renters. Owners can deduct interest paid on their mortgages (up to $750,000) and some local property taxes from their income subject to federal taxes. The size of these two subsidies—approximately $120 billion per year—dwarfs direct subsidies to low-income renters (around $40 billion). Academic research has debated whether homeownership creates wider social benefits: if homeowners take better care of their houses, are more engaged citizens, or are better parents. But the size of possible social benefits is nowhere near the scale of current subsidies.

Pitfall 3: Don't subsidize real estate over other wealth-building mechanisms.

Policymakers have clear reasons for encouraging households to accumulate savings. Savings insulate households against rainy days, allow them to invest in education, and pay for retirement. Housing is the largest financial asset for most households, so homeownership has been viewed as the primary mechanism of wealth-building.

But homeownership is also financially risky. By subsidizing owner-occupied housing more than other asset classes (such as stocks and bonds), current federal tax policy distorts households' incentives to build wealth through less risky and more diversified channels.

Conclusion

In the U.S., essential housing outcomes are largely determined by the invisible hand of the market—individual families negotiating with private-sector developers, landlords, and lenders. But public policy has the potential to improve the efficiency and equity of housing markets—if policies are thoughtfully designed and implemented. Having a clear idea of what goals housing policy should achieve is a necessary first step. Subsequent articles will address what current policies do, and how they could be improved.

Print Citations

CMS: Schuetz, Jenny. "Nine Rules for Better Housing Policy." In *The Reference Shelf: Affordable Housing*, edited by Micah L. Issit, 148-151. Amenia, NY: Grey House Publishing, 2019.

MLA: Schuetz, Jenny. "Nine Rules for Better Housing Policy." *The Reference Shelf: Affordable Housing*, edited by Micah L. Issit, Grey House Publishing, 2019, pp. 148-151.

APA: Schuetz, J. (2019). Nine rules for better housing policy. In Micah L. Issit (Ed.), *The reference shelf: Affordable housing* (pp. 148-151). Amenia, NY: Grey House Publishing.

Why Don't Homeless People Just Get Jobs?

By Kylyssa Shay
Soapboxie, January 14, 2019

Kylyssa Shay was homeless for over a year in her youth; it lead to her activism involving homelessness. She thinks, feels, and has opinions.

Why Don't Homeless People Just Get Jobs?

There are many assumptions about homeless people. Perhaps the most common is that they are too lazy to work. Having been there myself and having worked with many others in the same situation, I have to say that for the vast majority of homeless people, the assumption that they are lazy is dead wrong.

Many homed people look at the horrible lives of people living on the streets and ask why on earth a person wouldn't do something to help themselves in that situation. They ask, "Why don't they just get jobs?" Oddly enough, they don't seem to also wonder if jobs are available and if there are any barriers to getting a job without having a home or an address. "Why can't homeless people get jobs?" is a much better question.

I wrote this article to answer that question, to dispel a few more myths, and to drive home the reality that homelessness is something that no one asks for or deserves.

Why Can't Homeless People Get Jobs?

1. They don't have addresses, and most employers require addresses. This is a lose-lose situation: They can't get a place to live until they get a job, but can't get a job until they get a place to live.
2. Many employers won't consider unemployed job applicants (not even those with homes).
3. Many homeless people don't have reliable phones, and this becomes an obstacle to employment. Even if they have a phone, they might not always have a way to charge it.
4. It's hard to stay clean and neat when you're homeless, and most employers require grooming.

5. Many have gaps in their employment history, which is something that employers are suspicious about.
6. They have lousy credit scores. Many employers do credit screenings on potential employees, and when you're homeless, your credit score will suffer.
7. They don't have cars, and many jobs require one. Expensive transportation can be a huge obstacle to getting to work.
8. They have criminal records as a result of their homelessness (and sometimes, their only crime was not having a place to sleep).
9. Many are disabled. Many people with mental or physical disabilities end up on the street.
10. Addiction might play a part. Addictions prevent them from looking for work and from getting hired. Many employers assume homeless people are addicts.
11. Many have jobs already. Despite having a job, people still can still lose their homes or be unable to afford housing.

Each of these situations is described fully below, where you'll also find information about job statistics, how to help a homeless person get a job, and discussions about how easy it is to lose your home, whether or not homeless people are just lazy, and why money alone can't solve the problem.

1. Homeless People Don't Have Regular Addresses

This is pretty much the definition of being homeless. The lack of an address can be a huge obstacle to finding work. Many do not have a mailing address they can use on job applications or have the address to a PO box, church, or mission to use. Employers are put off by irregular addresses on job applications. **Don't kid yourself; many employers would never consider a homeless person for a job opening. They have the same misconceptions about them that everyone else does.** To get past this problem, some lie on applications or find a homed friend to provide an address for them, but this presents its own problems. If they catch this lie, most employers are less-than-understanding.

2. Some Employers Will Not Consider Unemployed Job Applicants

If your company downsizes and you become unemployed, you may be unable to find a job that accepts applications from people not currently working. Many job listings state that the unemployed should not apply. So even if you have a place to live and an address, if you are unemployed, you may have a harder time getting hired.

3. Many Don't Have Reliable Phones

It's hard to even have a charged mobile phone without somewhere to plug it in. Most employers won't even bother to figure out how to contact an applicant without a phone. This makes having a $25 pay-as-you-go phone a life saver for many. I've seen a number of people on the Internet complaining about homeless people with cell phones. Perhaps if they knew that a cell phone is often their only way to get a job, they might stop the complaining. Then again, maybe not.

4. It's Hard to Stay Clean and Neat When You're Homeless

The standard of cleanliness required of job applicants or employees can be unattainable for some. I've seen the suggestion that people just don't try hard enough to stay clean and well-groomed, but do you honestly think that you could show up to a job interview with a tidy haircut, a pressed suit and tie, shined shoes, a shower-fresh smell, and a clean shave without a home? For women, the situation is even harder due to social requirements to wear make-up.

5. Many Homeless People Have Gaps in Their Employment History

Employment gaps are unsurprising considering that such gaps in employment are often the cause of their homelessness. But still, most applications require an explanation for all gaps in employment, so the homeless person can either risk a lie or tell the truth and doom themselves. Even if the period of unemployment was caused by corporate downsizing, very few employers care to hear explanations.

6. Homeless People Have Lousy Credit Scores

Maintaining a great debt-to-income ratio is not easy when you live in a tent or some other unconventional place. In many states, it's perfectly legal for employers to run a credit screening on job applicants and disqualify those with poor credit ratings. As you can imagine, not having income leads to evictions and medical bankruptcies and past-due bills on your record, and this destroys your credit score. I doubt there are many, if any, homeless people with sterling credit ratings.

7. Many Homeless People Don't Have Cars

For some, it's a home-on-wheels, but many don't have even that. Many jobs require that applicants have dependable transportation. Sometimes this can be the bus, but if work hours are irregular and begin before buses start running or after they have stopped, it means owning your own vehicle. So not having a car or the money to pay bus fare means you can't get to work.

8. Many Homeless People Have Criminal Records

Homelessness, itself, is often a crime. In many cities in America, the state of being homeless is inherently illegal, so getting a criminal record is inevitable if one has nowhere to live in those areas. While some people on the street do commit crimes, sometimes their only crime is being without a place to sleep. It often doesn't take long for them to get criminal records without doing anything wrong. Charges for loitering, trespassing, unauthorized camping, or for falling asleep in a place not designated as a residence are common.

And since employers are turned off by criminal records, applicants without criminal records will almost always be preferred. Even if a homeless person lucks out and avoids getting a criminal record, he or she will often be assumed to be a criminal and an addict if their un-housed status is discovered.

9. Many Homeless People Are Disabled

By definition, disability is the inability to perform substantial work. Whether physically or mentally ill, many homeless people are disabled by their illnesses. I've read the criticisms and assertions that those with mental illness just need to straighten up and get a job. The problem is that anyone mentally ill enough to be sleeping in a cardboard box isn't fit to work a job until he or she gets at least a little better. They aren't faking; they aren't just being too lazy to work. Mentally ill homeless people are just that—mentally ill.

Do homeless people choose to be homeless?

How could anyone possibly think that sleeping outside, getting beaten and abused, and suffering humiliation after humiliation is preferable to working and having a safe, comfortable place to sleep, protection from assault, and respect from your fellow man? If a person really thought that the horror of homelessness was better than working a job, wouldn't that be pretty insane in itself? It's not a choice.

That strange, smelly homeless guy yelling nonsense at passersby is disabled by his mental illness. Some are physically too ill to hold down a job, too.

If people are disabled, then why aren't they living in a cheap apartment supported by Social Security Disability?

- They are often still in the process of applying for it. The first denial can take up to six months and the first appeal takes around 500 days. During that time, the physically disabled with nowhere to live are both unable to work and not getting any income.

- Also, to get Disability, applicants must be available to be contacted and able to make it to appointments, sometimes hundreds of miles away.

- Sometimes, getting Disability is impossible for homeless people. Being without an address might cause them to experience a delay too great in mail delivery making them disqualified to receive assistance for missing an appointment. Food assistance is often pretty much all they can get.

- Many of the mentally disabled who are living on the street are too messed up to get or hold down a job or sometimes even understand what is going on around them. If they are too disconnected or disaffected from reality to work a job, how on earth are they going to navigate the process of filing for Disability?

10. Addiction (and the Assumption of Addiction) Is an Obstacle to Employment

Not all homeless people are addicted to drugs, but most people believe that they are, including employers. Most people think this is the major reason homeless people don't get jobs, and it may be true for many chronically homeless people. Addictions prevent them from looking for work and from getting hired. However, the perception that all homeless people are drug-addicted criminals is possibly a greater barrier to their employment than actual drug addiction is. There's no doubt that addiction causes many people to remain homeless, but it is by no means the reason all homeless people are without homes or why they are not working.

11. Many Homeless People Have Jobs Already

One reason someone without housing may not be looking for a job is that he or she may already have a job or two already. Approximately a third to one half of the homeless population is employed. **Despite having a job, people can still lose their homes or be unable to afford housing.**

During the current economic situation, and with so many people un-housed due to mortgage foreclosures, in some cities well over half of the homeless population has jobs. Nationwide, the employment rate is about 44% for people without homes. Keeping in mind how many are elderly, children, disabled, or mentally ill that's a pretty high percentage.

Why don't these people have housing if they are employed?

- Many are working at minimum wage jobs which don't provide enough to pay for basic living expenses in many parts of the country.

- Many of them are underemployed; they don't get enough hours of work to pay the bills.

- Some people who work for low wages lose their homes when company cutbacks cut their hours.

There are working people all around you who are living in cars, in shelters, or on the street. In some cities like New York, even having full-time work is no guarantee of affordable housing.

So why don't they just get more work and work two or three jobs at a time?

Many of them do. But a cluster of minimum-wage jobs at a few hours a week doesn't generally get them very far. Getting enough hours with multiple jobs can be very difficult as well. To make multiple jobs work, employers have to be willing to work with a schedule that accommodates their employee's other jobs. Finding two (much less more) employers willing to work around other work schedules is difficult enough, but each added job makes finding and keeping a balance even more difficult. It is an extremely rare employer who is willing to schedule an employee around that employee's other job schedule.

I've worked as many as five part-time jobs at a time, which averaged me around a 65- to 70-hour work week. I had a home and a phone and it was still difficult to juggle the schedule. Eventually, I was forced to cut back to three jobs because of employers unwilling to work around other work schedules.

Homeless Employment Statistics

The fact that working a full-time job is not enough to house a person is a largely invisible problem due to a lack of data. This reality is not invisible to anyone who looks around their community and sees an increasing number of people living on the street or in their cars, but it is invisible to those who only believe the numbers. However, there are some numbers to look at:

- Researchers at the Urban Institute estimate that approximately 25% of the homeless population is employed.

- The National Coalition for the Homeless estimates that between 40 and 60% of homeless people shift in and out of full-time and part-time work.

- The Washington Council of Governments' 2017 report says that 22% of homeless, single adults and 25% of adults in homeless families are employed.

- The federal minimum wage is currently $7.25 per hour, but nationwide, an average hourly wage of $16.38 is required to rent an apartment.

- The population of working homeless is growing in cities across the US.

Money Alone Isn't Enough to Rent an Apartment

What?!? That's right, money alone is not enough to rent most apartments. To get into most apartment complexes in the United States, applicants must have a good credit score, good references, and have a job at which they earn at least three times as much as the monthly rent.

How much money do you need to make to rent an apartment?

While a person might be able to afford to rent an apartment working a minimum wage job by sticking to a very strict budget, still, most apartment complexes will not rent to him. A very modest one bedroom apartment might only cost $650 a month in budget housing but those who rent it must earn at least $1950 a month in most cases. Here in Michigan, a person

> **For the vast majority of homeless people, the assumption that they are lazy is dead wrong.**

earning the new, higher minimum wage of $9.45 an hour would still fall short by $438 per month. You'd need to earn at least $11.90 per hour to even be considered as an acceptable applicant for the apartment.

I recently helped friends fill out paperwork to move into a budget apartment complex and the requirement on their paperwork read that the rent must not exceed 30% of the applicants' combined income. So their $700 a month apartment requires them to earn at least $2,333 per month to be allowed to rent it.

Cosigners could help. Unfortunately, the combined income of the renter and the cosigner usually have to equal at least five times the monthly rent and the cosigner must not have a high debt-to-income ratio.

Are Homeless People Just Lazy?

You hear people claim that homeless people are just lazy, but can you imagine some-one saying to themselves, "I don't want to work. It's just no fun. I think I'd rather live on the street, exposed to the elements and violence." That makes no sense. There are many reasons for homelessness, but "lazy" is not on the list.

What are the main causes of homelessness?

- Low incomes and poverty.
- Lack of affordable housing.
- Unemployment.
- Family and relationship breakdowns.
- Domestic violence.
- Evictions and foreclosures.
- The affects of racial disparities.
- Disabilities and poor physical health.

How to Help a Homeless Person Get a Job

Even if you can't invite them to live with you, there are many things you can do to help.

- Hire them! If you have a job that fits their skills, give them a chance.
- If you know of any job opportunities, let them know. Ask around and do some legwork to help them connect with potential employers.
- Help them get, use, repair, and/or charge a phone.
- Help them set up and get to a job interview.
- Drive them to work (or help them pay for transportation).
- Let them use your address on their applications.
- Cosign to help them get an apartment (so they'll have an address to use on their application).
- Let them shower at your house.
- Let them wash their clothes in your machine.
- Give them some clean, work-appropriate clothing.
- Help them improve their credit scores.
- Help them get and take their medications.
- Help them access your local support organizations.
- Make sure they're eating properly.
- Be a friend. Listen to them and share your experience. Moral support helps, too!

How Easy Is It to Become Homeless?

If you ask how many people in the US are homeless now or how many people lose their homes each month, you won't be able to find firm figures. That's because most studies get their numbers by sporadically counting people who are in shelters or on specific streets at specific times, so those surveys underestimate the total number of people who are on the street today.

But no matter how imprecise the data is, one thing we do know is that homelessness is increasing at an alarming rate. Every day, it's getting easier and easier to lose everything and find yourself on the street . . . but if you fall into any of the following categories, your chance of becoming homeless increases:

- **If your wages don't keep up with inflation and cost of living increases.** In the 60s, a minimum-wage job could support a family of three, but that's no longer true today.

- **If you get laid off, downsized, or fired.** Loss of employment is one of the most common ways to lose housing.

- **If you lose your home.** In the last 10 years, home foreclosures have increased by over 30%, which also leads to an increase in evictions for renters.

- **If you get too old.** 50% of the homeless population is over the age of 50.

- **If you can't afford healthcare.** Medical costs a common reason for bankruptcy and poverty, and health problems or disabilities lead to homelessness.

- **If you are hit by a natural disaster.** Wildfires, hurricanes, and other natural disasters are on the rise, and those events usually precipitate housing crises.

- **If you are disabled.** More than 40% of the homeless population are people with disabilities, and this number keeps rising.

- **If you have mental health issues or issues with substance abuse.** Half of the people in shelters have either a substance use disorder, a psychiatric disorder, or both.

- **If you are a victim of domestic violence.** More than 80% of homeless mothers with children have experienced domestic violence.

- **If you serve in the military.** About 8% of the homeless population are veterans.

- **If you don't conform to gender or sexual norms**, you risk being kicked out of your home and losing familial support. In the US, more than 110,000 LGBTQ youth are homeless.

Print Citations

CMS: Shay, Kylyssa. "Why Don't Homeless People Just Get Jobs?" In *The Reference Shelf: Affordable Housing*, edited by Micah L. Issitt, 152-160. Amenia, NY: Grey House Publishing, 2019.

MLA: Shay, Kylyssa. "Why Don't Homeless People Just Get Jobs?" *The Reference Shelf: Affordable Housing*, edited by Micah L. Issit, Grey House Publishing, 2019, pp. 152-160.

APA: Shay, K. Why don't homeless people just get jobs? In Micah L. Issit (Ed.), *The reference shelf: Affordable housing* (pp. 152-160). Amenia, NY: Grey House Publishing.

Elizabeth Warren's New Housing Proposal Is Actually a Brilliant Plan to Close the Racial Wealth Gap

By Mehrsa Baradaran and Darrick Hamilton
Slate, October 26, 2018

Last month, Sen. Elizabeth Warren released a $450 billion housing plan called the American Housing and Economic Mobility Act. The proposal is a comprehensive and bold step toward providing affordable housing for the most vulnerable Americans. The bill is the first since the Fair Housing Act with the explicit intent of redressing the iterative effects of our nation's sordid history of housing discrimination. Critically, it has the potential to make a substantive dent in closing our enormous and persistent racial wealth gap.

Government discrimination played a big role in creating that gap. President Franklin D. Roosevelt's New Deal built an American middle class, but many programs were discriminatory in practice, bifurcating the nation into wealth-building white communities and segregated black communities. Most notoriously, the Home Owners' Loan Corporation and the Federal Housing Administration helped millions of white Americans buy homes but deliberately refused to insure mortgages for black families, particularly in white communities—a process known as redlining. Private lenders followed suit, refusing to provide loans to creditworthy borrowers, largely depriving the black community of mortgage credit and the opportunity to buy a home.

Over the next decades, white families used their home equity to secure small-business loans, send their children to college, or help their children put together home down payments—an iterative wealth building that was passed on to the next generation. In contrast, black families were left exposed to predatory private finance. Racially determined distribution of federal capital coupled with lending and housing discrimination begat an expanding racial wealth gap and decades of inter-generational poverty.

America's policies to redress these economic injustices have been largely insufficient. The Fair Housing Act—passed in the wake of the Rev. Martin Luther King, Jr.'s assassination in 1968—provided crucial legal protections against racial discrimination in housing, including the kinds of discriminatory practices that steered blacks away from high-amenity white neighborhoods toward high-poverty segregated ones—a common tactic of Northern segregationists. To promote deseg-regation, the bill gave the Department of Housing and Urban Development a strong mandate to "affirmatively further" the inclusion of black Americans in fair housing. But the bill failed to commit financial resources or drive capital into black neighborhoods to enable them to buy homes and close the gap from white communities who had enjoyed government support for decades.

As a result of this history, our nation still lives in the shadow of those fateful New Deal policies that were discriminatory in application. In America today, black children still suffer due to past segregation promoting housing policies that have confined blacks to low wealth and low asset appreciating ZIP codes. According to a recent report, 74 percent of neighborhoods that were redlined are still low income, and 64 percent are still minority neighborhoods.

Warren's bill is a monumental step forward that acknowledges injustice of the past and invests real money to redress it. Her bill would seek to address the racial wealth gap by establishing a down payment assistance program designed to support families who were historically excluded from government programs. The bill directs HUD to provide a grant that would be equivalent to an FHA loan down payment to all low- and middle-income first-time homebuyers who live in formerly redlined communities that are still low income. While many first-time homebuyers have help from family in putting together a down payment, government discrimination robbed most families in redlined neighborhoods of that opportunity. And so this provision has the potential to facilitate homeownership for hundreds of thousands of black families.

The bill also toughens the Community Reinvestment Act to force financial institutions to serve creditworthy families in communities they've ignored for decades. The bill expands the CRA to include nonbank mortgage lenders and credit unions who now provide more than half of mortgages; clarifies the law's requirement that institutions "serve" their communities, which have been subject to gaming by financial institutions; gives community groups more opportunities for input into regulators' evaluations of financial institutions; and requires regulators to disclose more of the data that informs their evaluations so that communities can assess whether investments that are supposed to support the community fulfill that promise. The bill encourages local jurisdictions to shed unnecessary laws—some of which were enacted shortly after the Fair Housing Act banned explicit exclusion of black families—that have made housing more expensive and prevented new residents from moving in. And it expands the Fair Housing Act itself to ban discrimination based on sexual orientation, gender identity or marital status, and source of income, including government benefits.

> **The legislation will help families buy affordable homes but also build asset security and community wealth by providing capital for down payments to those who have been historically excluded from homeownership.**

The American Housing and Economic Mobility Act also addresses the poverty caused by generations of housing discrimination. Black families are more likely to rent their homes because of historic exclusion from the housing market and restriction from accumulating and passing down wealth in general. In recent years, a severe shortage of affordable housing affecting every county in America has caused rents to spike for low- and middle-income renters, stretching their budgets and putting them at risk of eviction. The bill would invest $45 billion a year for 10 years in proven federal programs that use public capital to subsidize the construction and preservation of housing that's affordable to working families. An independent analysis by Moody's Analytics suggests this investment will produce more than 3 million new units and that new supply will pull down rents by 10 percent and create 1.5 million new jobs. In addition, the bill provides $2 billion in new grants to states to help homeowners and communities targeted with the most abusive loans before the financial crisis—often communities of color—where many homeowners still owe more on their mortgages than their properties are worth. These grants could be used for loan modifications that include principal reduction, purchasing or rehabilitation of vacant lots to increase neighborhood property values, or providing loans to negative equity borrowers to allow them to maintain or rehabilitate their homes.

All in all, the legislation will help families buy affordable homes but also build asset security and community wealth by providing capital for down payments to those who have been historically excluded from homeownership. It has the potential to lift historically marginalized communities by reversing more than a century of capital exclusion and housing discrimination. In a holistic way, Warren's bill attempts to address our past and ongoing housing problem by including targeted investments in rural communities, Native American communities, and formerly redlined black communities, echoing President Lyndon B. Johnson's War on Poverty and King's Poor People's movement.

The New Deal showed us the iterative and multigenerational value of wealth creation resulting from capital finance provided by government housing assistance. It is in this tradition that Warren is charting a way forward in which all Americans can have the economic security of having a roof over their heads.

Print Citations

CMS: Baradaran, Mehrsa, and Darrick Hamilton. "Elizabeth Warren's New Housing Proposal Is Actually a Brilliant Plan to Close the Racial Wealth Gap." In *The Reference Shelf: Affordable Housing*, edited by Micah L. Issit, 161-163. Amenia, NY: Grey House Publishing, 2019.

MLA: Baradaran, Mehrsa, and Darrick Hamilton. "Elizabeth Warren's New Housing Proposal Is Actually a Brilliant Plan to Close the Racial Wealth Gap." *The Reference Shelf: Affordable Housing,* edited by Micah L. Issit, Grey House Publishing, 2019, pp. 161-163.

APA: Baradaran, M., & D. Hamilton. (2019). Elizabeth Warren's new housing proposal is actually a brilliant plan to close the racial wealth gap. In Micah L. Issit (Ed.), *The reference shelf: Affordable housing* (pp. 161-163). Amenia, NY: Grey House Publishing.

Bibliography

"Affordable Housing." *HUD*. Housing and Urban Development. 2018. Retrieved from https://www.hud.gov/program_offices/comm_planning/affordablehousing/.

Anzilotti, E. "This Plan Shows How Government Should Get Back in the Housing Business." *Fast Company*. Jul 24, 2018. Retrieved from https://www.fastcompany.com/90204034/this-plan-shows-how-government-should-get-back-in-the-housing-business.

Biles, Roger. *From Tenements to Taylor Homes: In Search of an Urban Housing Policy in Twentieth-Century America*. University Park: The Pennsylvania University Press, 2000.

Calhoun, Michael. "Lessons from the Financial Crisis: The Central Importance of a Sustainable, Affordable and Inclusive Housing Market." *Brookings*. The Brookings Institution. Sep 5, 2018. Retrieved from https://www.brookings.edu/research/lessons-from-the-financial-crisis-the-central-importance-of-a-sustainable-affordable-and-inclusive-housing-market/.

Childs, Richard S. "What Is a House?" in Whitaker, Ackerman, Child, and Wood, eds., *The Housing Problem in War and in Peace*. Washington, DC: Journal of the American Institute of Architects, 1918.

Covert, Bryce. "All of a Sudden, Politicians Are Ready to Tackle America's Housing Crisis." *The Nation*. Nov 20, 2018. Retrieved from https://www.thenation.com/article/affordable-housing-crisis-warren-booker-harris/.

Daugherty, Owen. "Homelessness Rates Increase for Second Straight Year." *The Hill*. Dec 17, 2018. Retrieved from https://thehill.com/blogs/blog-briefing-room/news/421684-homelessness-rates-increase-in-us-for-second-straight-year.

"Defining Housing Affordability." *Huduser.com*. 2018. Retrieved from https://www.huduser.gov/portal/pdredge/pdr-edge-featd-article-081417.html.

Demby, Gene. "For People of Color, a Housing Market Partially Hidden from View." *NPR*. National Public Radio. Jun 17, 2013. Retrieved from https://www.npr.org/sections/codeswitch/2013/06/17/192730233/for-people-of-color-a-housing-market-partially-hidden-from-view.

Desilver, Drew. "For Most U.S. Workers, Real Wages Have Barely Budged in Decades." *Pew Research*. Aug 7, 2018. Retrieved from http://www.pewresearch.org/fact-tank/2018/08/07/for-most-us-workers-real-wages-have-barely-budged-for-decades/.

Desmond, Matthew. "Americans Want to Believe Jobs Are the Solution to Poverty. They're Not." *The New York Times*. The New York Times Co. Sep 11, 2018. Retrieved from https://www.nytimes.com/2018/09/11/magazine/americans-jobs-poverty-homeless.html.

Edson, Charles L. "Affordable Housing—An Intimate History." *Journal of Affordable*

Housing and Community Development Law. Winter 2011. Retrieved from http://apps.americanbar.org/abastore/products/books/abstracts/5530024%20chapter%201_abs.pdf.

Epstein, Richard A. "The Affordable Housing Crisis." *Hoover Institution*. Feb 27, 2017. Retrieved from https://www.hoover.org/research/affordable-housing-crisis.

Florida, Richard. "How Affordable Housing Can Improve the American Economy." *CityLab*. Feb 5, 2019. Retrieved from https://www.citylab.com/life/2019/02/affordable-housing-economy-city-zoning-home-prices/582022/.

Furman, Jason. "Barriers to Shared Growth: The Case of Land Use Regulation and Economic Rents. *Obama White House*. Nov 20, 2015. Retrieved from https://obamawhitehouse.archives.gov/sites/default/files/page/files/20151120_barriers_shared_growth_land_use_regulation_and_economic_rents.pdf.

Goodman, Laurie, McCargo, Alanna, and Jun Zhu. "A Closer Look at the Fifteen-Year Drop in Black Homeownership." *Urban Institute*. Urban Wire. Feb 12, 2018. Retrieved from https://www.urban.org/urban-wire/closer-look-fifteen-year-drop-black-homeownership.

Hobbes, Michael. "America's Housing Crisis Is a Ticking Time Bomb." *Huffington Post*. June 19, 2018. Retrieved from https://www.huffingtonpost.com/entry/housing-crisis-inequality-harvard-report_us_5b27c1f1e4b056b2263c621e.

Hughes, Becky. "Working Homeless Population Grows in Cities Across the U.S." *Parade*. AMG/Parade. Feb 7, 2018. Retrieved from https://parade.com/643064/beckyhughes/working-homeless-population-grows-in-cities-across-the-u-s/.

Kneebone, Elizabeth, Snyderman, Robin, and Cecile Murray. "Advancing Regional Solutions to address America's Housing Affordability Crisis." *Brookings*. The Avenue. Oct 23, 2017. Retrieved from https://www.brookings.edu/blog/the-avenue/2017/10/19/advancing-regional-solutions-to-address-americas-housing-affordability-crisis/.

Ligon, John. "Federal Reforms Should Include Housing and Land-Use Deregulation." *Heritage*. The Heritage Foundation. Mar 28, 2018. Retrieved from https://www.heritage.org/housing/report/federal-reforms-should-include-housing-and-land-use-deregulation.

Madrigal, Alexis C. "The Racist Housing Policy That Made Your Neighborhood." *The Atlantic*. The Atlantic Monthly Group. May 22, 2014.

Martens, Betsey. "A Political History of Affordable Housing." *Journal of Housing & Community Development*. January/February 2009. Retrieved from http://content.csbs.utah.edu/~fan/fcs5400-6400/studentpresentation2009/03Reading_3.pdf.

Matthews, Dylan. "The Case against Tiny Houses." *Vox*. Vox Media. Sep 26, 2016. Retrieved from https://www.vox.com/a/new-economy-future.

Meck, Stuart, Retzlaff, Rebecca, and James Schwab. "Regional Approaches to Affordable Housing." *American Planning Association*. 2002. https://www.huduser.gov/Publications/PDF/regional_app_aff_hsg.pdf.

Milkman, Arielle. "The Tiny House Fantasy." *Jacobin*. Jan 19, 2016. https://www.

jacobinmag.com/2016/01/tiny-house-movement-nation-tumbleweed-environ-ment-consumerism/.

Plunkett, Mike. "Tiny Houses Amid Big Issues as Communities Tackle Homeless-ness." *The Washington Post*. Oct 26, 2018. Retrieved from https://www.washing-tonpost.com/graphics/2018/national/tiny-houses/.

Reeves, Richard V. and Dimitrios Halikias. "How Land Use Regulations Are Zoning Out Low Income Families." *Brookings Institute*. Social Mobility Memos. Aug 16, 2016. Retrieved from https://www.brookings.edu/blog/social-mobility-mem-os/2016/08/16/zoning-as-opportunity-hoarding/

Reinicke, Carmen. "US Income Inequality Continues to Grow." *CNBC*. CNBC. Jul 19, 2018. Retrieved from https://www.cnbc.com/2018/07/19/income-inequali-ty-continues-to-grow-in-the-united-states.html.

Rogers, Adam. "Big Tech Isn't the Problem with Homelessness. It's All of Us." *Wired*. Condé Nast. Jun 21, 2018. Retrieved from https://www.wired.com/story/big-tech-isnt-the-problem-with-homelessness-its-all-of-us/.

Rowe, Michael and Charles Barber. "The Power of Giving Homeless People a Place to Belong." *CityLab*. Jun 12, 2018.

Schneider, Benjamin. "CityLab Universisty: Inclusionary Zoning." *CityLab*. Jul 17, 2018. Retrieved from https://www.citylab.com/equity/2018/07/citylab-universi-ty-inclusionary-zoning/565181/.

Schneider, Benjamin. "The American Housing Crisis Might Be Our Next Big Po-litical Issue." *CityLab*. May 16, 2018. Retrieved from https://www.citylab.com/equity/2018/05/is-housing-americas-next-big-political-issue/560378/.

Shoag, Daniel. "Removing Barriers to Accessing High Productivity Places." *The Brookings Institution*. Jan 31, 2019. Retrieved from https://www.brookings.edu/research/removing-barriers-to-accessing-high-productivity-places/.

"The Silent Crisis in America." *Home1*. Public Interest. 2018. Retrieved from http://home.one/about/#grve-scrolling-section-5c5b4da37e77b.

Sisson, Patrick. "The Housing Crisis Isn't Just about Affordability—It's about Eco-nomic Mobility, Too." *Curbed*. Vox Media. Apr 24, 2018. Retrieved from https://www.curbed.com/2018/4/24/17275068/jobs-mobility-high-rent-housing-costs.

Sisson, Patrick. "Solving Affordable Housing: Creative Solutions around the U.S." *Curbed*. Vox Media. Jul 25, 2017. Retrieved from https://www.curbed.com/2017/7/25/16020648/affordable-housing-apartment-urban-development.

Sisson, Patrick. "Tiny Houses: Big Future, or Big Hype?" *Curbed*. Jul 18, 2017. Re-trieved from https://www.curbed.com/2017/7/18/15986818/tiny-house-zoning-adu-affordable-housing.

Sommeiller, Estelle and Mark Price. *The Increasingly Unequal States of America: Income Inequality by State, 1917 to 2011*. Economic Analysis and Research Net-work (EARN). Feb 19, 2014.

Stevens, Glenn. "Affordable Housing: The Crisis No One Is Talking About." *NCHM*. National Center for Housing Management. Apr 8, 2016. Retrieved from http://www.nchm.org/Resources/Compliance-Corner/Review/ArticleId/140/Afford-able-housing-the-crisis-no-one-is-talking-about.

Tanzi, Alexandre. "Top 3% of U.S. Taxpayers Paid Majority of Income Tax in 2016." *Bloomberg*. Oct 14, 2018. Retrieved from https://www.bloomberg.com/news/articles/2019-02-07/trump-says-he-s-open-to-changing-salt-deduction-cap-in-tax-law.

Uhlfelder, Eric. "How Cities Should Take Care of Their Housing Problem." *The New York Times*. The New York Times Co. Feb 21, 2017. Retrieved from https://www.nytimes.com/2017/02/21/opinion/how-cities-should-take-care-of-their-housing-problems.html.

Von Hoffman, Alexander. "To Preserve Affordable Housing in the United States: A Policy History." *JCHS*. Joint Center for Housing Studies. March 2016. Retrieved from http://www.jchs.harvard.edu/sites/default/files/von_hoffman_to_preserve_affordable_housing_april16.pdf.

Wiltz, Teresa. "As Affordable Housing Crisis Deepens, States Begin to Take Action." *CS Monitor*. Oct 16, 2018. Retrieved from https://www.csmonitor.com/Business/2018/1016/As-affordable-housing-crisis-deepens-states-begin-to-take-action.

Yglesias, Matthew. "Elizabeth Warren's Proposed Tax on Enormous Fortunes, Explained." *Vox*. Vox Media. Jan 24, 2019. Retrieved from https://www.vox.com/policy-and-politics/2019/1/24/18196275/elizabeth-warren-wealth-tax.

Zestos, George K. *The Global Financial Crisis: From US Subprime Mortgages to European Sovereign Debt*. New York: Routledge, 2016.

Websites

Brookings Institution
www.brookings.edu

The Brookings Institution is a nonprofit public policy thinktank located in Washington DC. Brookings scholars have researched and written about housing, economic inequality, and American history and studies available through the Brookings website provide a valuable resource for studying the housing crisis and many other economic and social welfare issues in America.

CityLab
www.citylab.com

CityLab is a web magazine published by the Atlantic Monthly Group that focuses on issues affecting cities both in the United States and around the world. Co-founded by urban theorist Richard Florida, the magazine covers urban development, crime, municipal politics and housing issues. Journalists publishing articles through *CityLab* have covered many different aspects of the affordable housing debate.

Department of Housing and Urban Development (HUD)
www.hud.gov

The Department of Housing and Urban development is the branch of the federal government responsible for formulating and directing federal responses to housing issues across the United States. HUD provides information on a variety of housing issues and publishes reports on issues involving houses, including homelessness, the state of the housing market, real estate trends, and other federal programs.

Joint Center for Housing Studies (JCHS)
www.jchs.harvard.edu

The Joint Center for Housing Studies is a department within Harvard University that helps to research and develop proposals for housing reform. Founded in 1959, the organization also publishes an annual report on the state of the housing market, supports research into economic and social issues and policies, and offers training for individuals interested in urban studies, planning, and development.

National Alliance to End Homelessness

www.endhomelessness.org

The National Alliance to End Homelessness is a Washington DC.-based advocacy organization that provides access to data and research on homelessness and related issues, including affordable housing, income inequality, and economic outreach. The organization funds research, creates policy proposals, and works with local and community organizations to create homelessness programs in various regions.

National Coalition for the Homeless

www.nationalhomeless.org

The National Coalition for the Homeless is an online network of advocates, activists, and service organizations focused on addressing homelessness in the United States. The organization provides access to research and academic resources as well as practical public resources for individuals experiencing homelessness or housing insecurity.

National Low Income Housing Coalition (NLIHC)

www.nlihc.org

The National Low Income Housing Coalition is a non-profit lobbyist organization headquartered in Washington DC. that focuses on issues surrounding housing and social welfare. The organization funds and publishes report on the state of US housing, develops policy recommendations for state and federal agencies, and provides a variety of information available to the public, such as a directory of homeless shelters and housing outreach organizations in each state.

Urban Institute

www.urban.org

The Urban Institute is a Washington DC-based think tank focused on economic and social welfare research. Founded in 1968, the Urban Institute conducts studies on municipal policies, develops policy recommendations, and researchers issues impacting the lives of urban residents, such as housing, economic inequality, suburban sprawl, and penal system rehabilitation.

Index